The
Management
Of

Commercial
Computing

Dr Andreas Sofroniou

Andreas Sofroniou

My thanks to my family

for all their patience

and support.

Andreas

Andreas Sofroniou

Andreas Sofroniou © Copyrights.

ISBN: 0 9527956 0 4

Copyright © Andreas Sofroniou

1996

Published and Printed by:

PsySys Limited

33, SN3 1PH, UK.

1996

FOREWORD

There can be little doubt that information systems and computing in general, will become increasingly important in the years ahead. This book is, therefore, aiming to fill a gap in the current business and tutorial literature.

The Business Information Systems book has been designed for the business person, for the student and the computer professional who needs a detailed overview of Information Technology and the systems involved.

The book explores the fundamental aspects of operational computing, the development of new information systems, the choice of packages and the structured methodologies used. Current systems are discussed according to their structure and the book focuses on further developments in information technology, the year 2000 compliance and their planning.

In writing the book, the author is mostly concerned with the development and the managing of systems and people in multi-national corporations, software houses, government departments, the European Union Commissions and academia.

EurIng Dr Andreas Sofroniou has close links with business systems and their development, as well as the system engineering profession as a whole. He has developed numerous systems and managed a variety of applications and systems people, including Year 2000 projects.

It is the author's wish that the reader thoroughly enjoys reading the contents of this book.

Andreas Sofroniou

Contents

Preface

This book is mostly concerned with the development and the management of systems and the people involved in such development. The individuals who work on their own and those who work in groups to design systems applicable to users. The system practitioners who may be employed by multi-national corporations, software houses, government departments, European Union Commissions, or academia.

Computing as a service is given to all types of businesses, in any environment. As a tool at work, a systems department deals with individual problems, ranging from difficulties within job responsibilities, rifts and business inadequacies, including systems, operational problems and the people involved in such activities.

The book will assist operational groups of people, in various sections of commercial computing. Based on the contents, training courses can be prepared to suit the candidates, mainly workshops concerned with human-computer interactions, systems development and systems methodologies.

The modern Information Technology Executive attempts to merge the latest developments in human sciences and advanced technology. The combination of both, gives a service applicable to the systems user and his/her working surroundings.

In computing, the major theme is the responsibility to the system user, the individual and the company; to help with their problems and requirements in system development. The emergent technologies and the pace of change are placing increasing importance upon organisations and individuals being finely tuned, in performance terms. This does not just happen, but has to be worked at.

The Information Technology Manager's role is to provide a service in computing which will assist in developing skills, diagnose and treat discontinuities which affect the performance of the systems. In computing, the commercial, industrial and human expertise embrace the whole range of services. Technology in business environments, directing and management techniques, systems designing, personnel selection, counselling, training and individual development, production methods and artificial intelligence.

Many organisational and personnel problems may be solved. The system engineer offers advice and undertakes assignments relating to all aspects of information technology, including strategic, business and data analysis, systems and database designing, networking, hardware and software selection and systems users training. Within an organisation, the computing expertise can be offered as an ad-hoc advisory service, as a short term systems specialist, or on a long term project basis.

This book will prove very useful to the Executive who wishes to use modern skills, such as the human aspects of system management and directing, setting of tasks, project management and the state-of-the-art in computing, as a tool.

The responsibilities within information technology and the systems engineering areas, include the understanding of user personality, human-computer interaction and comparative methods within structured systems designing.

On the academic, educational and training aspect, the importance of a person as a whole system engineering professional must be emphasised, this being the major factor in dealing with organisational, system and personal problems. In the last few years, modern universities prepare their courses to suit the business environment and towards the professional accreditation of the appropriate computing institution and the engineering council. The whole venture of academia and the engineering institutions is seen by businesses as a pro for a continuous human development policy. This ensures high quality employment opportunities, secured in growth industries at the forefront of technological changes.

THE MANAGEMENT OF COMMERCIAL COMPUTING

1: Background

1.1   Introduction

In the past, the majority of data processing has been carried out by companies using batch style computer systems. With the cost of hardware rapidly reducing and with the hardware power and facilities increasing inversely, on-line systems are now becoming easier to justify and develop.

The objectives of data processing are to capture data, process it and present the information. Because of the widespread use of computers within business, it is sometimes assumed that data always refers to some type of financially oriented transaction.

In fact, data has a more general meaning. In general terms, data can be used to denote any or all facts, numbers, letters and symbols that refer to, or describe an object, idea, condition, or any other function. But data can only be of value if it can be organised in some way, so that it becomes meaningful to somebody - this is information.

The data must be checked for integrity, to ensure that errors have not arisen during any data capture processes. Data are compared to establish relationships, similarities and differences. By now the data should have been completely processed, but to be proper information the processing results must be presented in such a way that it has relevance and meaning. Finally, the information must be produced on a medium that is legible.

In years bygone, on-line systems of any form have been difficult to justify because of the cost of:

- additional hardware needed to sustain speedy response times,
- systems software needed to support individual terminal activity,
- additional design overhead for systems assurance.

With hardware power increasing and their costs reducing rapidly, these objectives are now disappearing.

Indeed, the justification for modern applications must be much easier now, when their benefits include:

- speedier data entry,
- reduced data error rates,
- faster processing cycles,
- quick response to user enquiries.

1.2   Background of Information Systems

Of all the major problems encountered in computing, the most difficult is the management of the systems and their development. Unlike any engineering or architectural drawings, the systems cannot be visibly represented as a model. Any building or machine can be shown as a set of drawings and as a three dimensional model, but the design and the build of the system cannot be seen, nor can it be represented on top of a desk.

In the case of an architectural concept, the designer will draw the plans and will supervise and delegate the tasks to builders to construct in a fashion, as close to perfect logistics as possible.

In modern computing, structured methodologies are used, where dataflow diagrams can be drawn, data can be modelled and at the end of the logical phase, the system can be prototyped and programmed.

This brings forward the problem of managing, delegating, and guiding those who analyse the business requirements and the data on which the information is based, the professionals who proceed with the design based on the requirements and those who program and implement the required system.

In most cases, these activities are under one roof. Mainly, three different professions passing details to each other at the end of each developmental stage; Analysis, Designing and Programming. The Information Technology Manager will need to know what each step of development involves and at every phase what the professional system engineer is doing. As in every other project, tasks need to be based on timescales and the financial implication to remain close to the budgets.

In commercial computing the financial costs for developing a new system are in six figures and in many cases where additional hardware and software are to be acquired, one project can be in the region of millions of pounds. To cope with such enormities of resources and the correct availability of business information, an organisation relies completely on the professional knowledge of its system engineers and those who manage the projects.

The media frequently report failures of systems and frustrations in computers at large. More often within companies, disappointments in systems are such that
the computer department is totally isolated from other business activities. Yet, there are those companies whose total running of their business is based on the smooth running of their computer systems. The profitability and the revenue always ahead of their competitors.

But, it is also true to say that with all modern computing and devices, industry still suffers, or outputs could be improved, if only the computer department could design and operate a system the way the users work and based on the company's requirements.

The systems person is aware of these problems and yet cannot stretch his/her know-how any more than is already done. Imagine the various professionals under one roof, the complexity of designing and constructing systems, of the housekeeping involved, of the running and maintenance of all these sections.

If an organisation has many departments to enable it to function, so does the computer environment. In a superimposed mode, the Information Technology Manager has just as many sections to look after, admittedly on a smaller scale, but just as complex. Humans, machines, finances, stresses, productions, outputs, man-machine relationships, all in one department, just as much as any overall organisation is facing.

The I.T. Manager relies on management skills, systems knowledge and various other business methods in order to give a good service to everybody in the company. The subject covers business computing and its management, the development of new systems, the implementation and their running. The Manager in computing is aware of actual examples and will draw on projects and experience gained in building large and moderate systems based on what the users require, their problems, the solutions and their training in ensuring the success of the new system, or additional information technology modules.

In the first place, the expertise of those involved must cover the last generation of computing (which systems are still operating in many international organisations), its successes and its failures and the running in company environments. This includes the mainframe-based systems, the advent of PCs (Personal Computers) and their impact on networking and distributed processing, expert systems, shells and artificial intelligence.

These, inevitably will be supported by training and experience in Structured Methodologies, a comparative study into methods, the use of the predominant systems architectures and a method for 'Rapid Building' system engineering.

In the U.K. the structured methodology most of the systems people follow is
the Government and Defence companies preferred SSADM (Structured System Analysis and Design Methodology) version 4. Almost entirely, all the western organisations who create new systems use a structured methodology. The analysis of the logical stages, the use of CASE (Computer-aided Software Engineering) tools and the consideration of COTS, (Commercial Off The Shelf) systems, including GOTS (Government Off The Shelf) packages.

Modern systems engineering, concentrates on the training aspect, the psychology of users, motivation and delegating specific to the computer departments, the interviewing techniques in gathering the information on current systems, the cataloguing of the problems and requirements, the appropriate solutions and their incorporation into the design of the required system.

Regarding the newcomers to the commercial computing professions, organisations rely on aspiring young graduates. With all good will they bring with them and with all their ambitions for the yuppie incomes, graduates still need the specialised training in computing and systems applications to business requirements.

It must be said that academia has progressed enormously in computing during the last ten years, but business needs differ from that of university research and studies. Graduates who enter the companies surroundings find that they are unprepared for the demand of creating and using commercial systems in large organisations.

1.3   Computer Background

The early electronic computers of the 1940s had central processing units built up of banks of vacuum tubes, 'the glass bottles', also found in old wireless sets and television receivers. The CPUs (Central Processing Units), needed thousands of these tubes. The systems were cumbersome and unreliable, only hours between failures. There were heavy electrical power demands and the cooling plant was often as large as the computer.

The first computer of this type was ENIAC (Electronic Numerical Integrator and Computer), developed in the USA by J P Eckert and JW Mauchmy. ENIAC completed by 1946, was designed with the purpose of generating artillery firing tables. Built up of 18,000 vacuum tubes; it was immense, requiring a room 60 feet by 25 feet to hold it and weighing more than 30 tons.

In 1948, a transistor was first demonstrated by William Shockley, John Bardeen and Walter Brattain, working in the Bell Telephone Laboratory, in the USA. Transistors could do virtually all the jobs of the then conventional vacuum tube valves, but required much less electrical power, generated very little heat and were much smaller. They were considerably more reliable and made possible the development of computers as effective functional devices in an increasingly wide range of applications.

The computers of the fifties and early sixties, individually used thousands of transistors. The various electronic components, transistors, resistors, capacitors and diodes were mounted on printed circuit cards or boards. Copper was selectively edged from phenolic or fibreglass base to leave electrical connections between holes in which the wires of the components were inserted. A typical five-inch square printed circuit card would contain about a dozen transistors and a hundred or so other components.

Each computer (now second generation) comprised several thousand printed circuit cards. The cards, regarded as modules, were slotted into frames and interconnected by means of back-wiring. A typical large computer would be built up from several dozen specific modules, each of them being used up to several times in each computer.

In the sixties, the semi-conductor makers created a whole new technology, making possible the development of third generation computers. Using a more sophisticated version of transistor fabrication technology, it was possible to manufacture dozens of transistors together on a single small silicon chip. In this way an electronic circuit previously comprising many separate inter-connected components, could be manufactured as a single integrated unit.

By the early seventies, the basic components, transistors, diodes, etc. were assembled in a ten micro-millimetre thick surface layer in a silicon wafer. The components were then connected by metal layer evaporated on to the silicon. Subsequent etching produced a required inter-connection. Several of the integrated circuits could be mounted on a printed circuit card which could carry all the circuitry necessary for a central processing unit and the associated computer elements.

In recent years, integrated circuits were manufactured with a complexity of around one thousand transistors. The first micro-processor, produced by Intel Corporation in 1971, was based on a single quarter of an inch silicon chip which carried the equivalent of 2,250 transistors, all the necessary CPU circuitry for a tiny computer. By 1976, chips of this size using LSI (Large Scale Integration) could carry more than 20,000 components. Looking into the early part of the next millennium, the chip fabrication will allow larger chips to be built using smaller technology.

When a computer CPU is one integrated circuit, or a small number of circuits, the CPU is called a micro-processor. A micro-processor used with other integrated components forms a micro-computer.

The latest introduction of Intel's Pentium range, Motorola's and other manufacturers' equivalent PC-based capacity and speed, together with the personal computers software such as the Microsoft hold users in amazement and difficulty in following the development in computing.

THE MANAGEMENT OF COMMERCIAL COMPUTING

In general, all modern computers and Personal Computers (PCs) have similar architecture features, functional elements equivalent to those of a large mainframe. The PCs may vary in performance according to their storage capacity. However, these are encroaching on many application areas, formerly the exclusive province of the larger computers.

The cost of computer hardware is expected to fall during the late nineties and it is expected that the resident software will be given free as part of the PC. Application software, in a packaged form and helpful in running commercial systems, will be of minimal cost.

Today, PCs are affecting work and leisure alike, increasingly involved in factory and business operations, networking, defence, medicine, education and the domestic environment. They are influencing attitudes to privacy, employment and other social issues.

2: Systems Engineering

2.1 The Diagrammatic Representation Of Systems

The reader must remember that the construction of a system is as complex as a house built in a swamp. It requires careful planning and design. Just as a house must have an architect's plan, so does a system. It must have requirements, system objectives and a blueprint.

In general, it must be well noticed that every system structured is an answer to the users problems and requirements. The solutions will be based on the studies of the current systems, manual and computerised and the problems and requirements catalogue.

The design of the system will be based on how the users work and what suits the overall business environment. Whilst analysing the users needs, the system engineer will proceed with the logical stages, by listening, interviewing and having Walkthroughs and reviews with users and colleagues.

Prior to proceeding into the physical stages, the system engineers and managers involved, will seek approval from the appropriate groups of people. Within the physical stages and during the construction of the system, the system builders will test and make the necessary alterations to the modules being implemented.

The users systems acceptance will include all the necessary documentation and all the training and support required to ensure that the new system, or module is successful.

The illustration of the overall computing environment, (on the following page) can help in unravelling these complexities. The hierarchical diagram represents computing in large organisations. Within IT five major modules are included in a structured mode. Every module is diagrammatically represented, at different levels.

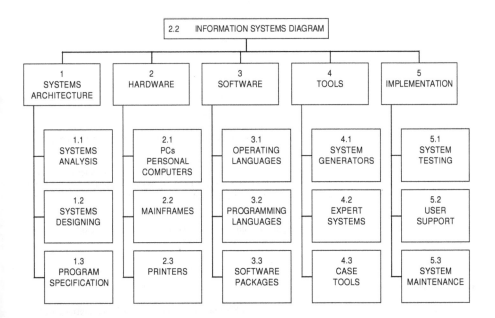

2.2   INFORMATION SYSTEMS DIAGRAM

1 SYSTEMS ARCHITECTURE	2 HARDWARE	3 SOFTWARE	4 TOOLS	5 IMPLEMENTATION
1.1 SYSTEMS ANALYSIS	2.1 PCs PERSONAL COMPUTERS	3.1 OPERATING LANGUAGES	4.1 SYSTEM GENERATORS	5.1 SYSTEM TESTING
1.2 SYSTEMS DESIGNING	2.2 MAINFRAMES	3.2 PROGRAMMING LANGUAGES	4.2 EXPERT SYSTEMS	5.2 USER SUPPORT
1.3 PROGRAM SPECIFICATION	2.3 PRINTERS	3.3 SOFTWARE PACKAGES	4.3 CASE TOOLS	5.3 SYSTEM MAINTENANCE

2.3   Systems Architecture

The background of structured analysis and designing as an information engineering methodology, a technique-driven approach, started in 1972. Between 1980 and 1982, Gane and Sarson and Yourdon methodologies were extensively used. In 1983, business started using the information engineering automated version. By 1989, the information engineering development paths underwent further evolution. In 1992, the business re-engineering and object-oriented versions were introduced.

The need to control and manage the ever-increasing amounts of all organisational data being created, particularly computer-generated data, has gained recognition. However, because data management automates the processes used within a company, implementation is not easy. Several data management suppliers have begun requesting that a full systems and business analysis is undertaken prior to system implementation.

This shows not only where existing processes need to be changed but determines exactly what the data management system needs to do within each unique organisation. It, therefore, provides the platform for successful systems architecture and management introduction and avoids the many pitfalls that so many companies have experienced in attempting to develop and install a new management system.

Rapid prototyping is gaining acceptance. Companies are using this method to obtain system design models in weeks rather than months, dramatically reducing lead-times and enabling better decisions and choice of system modules to be made.

A Systems Engineer in his/her approach defines the whole project, modularises it into manageable sections and proceeds in a logical manner according to the clear principles of user involvement.

The tasks are always broken down into a structured. goal-oriented, meaningful units of work. The end result of these structured sets of tasks are applicable to the development path of:

- Information Strategy Planning,
- Business Area Analysis,
- Business Design/Technical Design,
- Construction,
- Transition,
- Production.

The above stages can be used by Analysts, Designers, Project Managers, Directors and Trainers in information technology methods to suit the technical and the user environment.

New techniques have been introduced that dramatically reduce the time taken to solve business and system problems. The result is that it is now possible to take the requirements, analyse and view the results in days or weeks, rather than months. This, of course, makes analysis possible and cost-effective within the design process, rather than a special system task.

Recent years have seen further development in business and systems analysis software. Product releases of leading software houses, have not only made systems architecture easier for everyday system engineers, but faster too. Closer links to CASE (Computer-aided Software Engineering) systems have made analysis simpler, while new interfaces make analysis understandable to users.

The term systems analysis is used in many computer installations in different ways. In fact, for most development projects it means the following:

- fact finding,
- operational analysis,
- business system design.

System analysis for an organisation means that the analyst has more detailed work to do by establishing with the users that there is a justification for developing a new system.

2.4   Designing Systems

The interface between the user and a computer system has always been an important design factor. In interactive computer systems the interface (the dialogue) can influence not only the system's efficiency, but also its acceptability to the user.

The significance of effective dialogue design has its advantages and disadvantages:

- computer initiated dialogues are initially effective for the novice user, but quickly fall into disfavour when the user becomes more familiar with the system,
- equally, 'short-hand' user initiated dialogues can only be used effectively by an experienced user.

Therefore, the first aspect of interface design is to determine who will be using the system and how frequently they will be using it.

It may be necessary to have two sets of dialogues for the same system. One for the trainees and a 'short-hand' version for experienced staff.

The user psychology here is extremely important. The interface between the user and the system must be an extension of the way the user does his/her work. Any dialogue which causes deviation from this, will cause frustration and ultimately dislike for the system.

The second aspect of dialogue design is to ensure that the system is friendly and responsive.

Friendly means that:

- the screen formats are easy to read, data entry areas are clearly identified and error conditions are highlighted,
- the computer displays messages on the screens giving the status of user initiated functions.

Responsive means that the computer should react to a user's request within a given response time, which is normally a low number of seconds.

In summary, the design of the system is significant because:

- it affects the character of the overall systems design,
- it directly affects user acceptability,
- once committed to a design it is expensive to change.

The new technology is introducing techniques which are changing the way organisations work, as opposed to just addressing existing tasks. To successfully implement and apply the systems tools requires extensive education and it is this that is currently presenting the biggest hurdles for companies.

2.5   Security and System Assurance

Computer security has become a challenge dominated by the improvements to the technology of computers. Techniques are being developed to make access to systems harder. In recent years, much work has been done to make the computer recognise individual characteristics, unique to the user, such as a signature, a fingerprint, or even the genetic print of DNA.

With users and companies becoming more dependent upon computer systems, the privacy and reliability of such systems are becoming critical aspects of design. Systems Assurance, a term which is currently popular, of a system embraces the parts of systems design which reduce the risk of both the fraudulent use of the system and lengthly recovery times in the event of a system's failure.

In many companies, one of the few problems that has to be resolved quickly, is:

- privacy, the fraudulent entry of data,
- policing, a system must be more than reporting violation, it must include effective restricted access at varying levels, to different users,
- recording access violations.

Users and companies are becoming more and more dependent upon resilience of computer-based systems. Computer systems can fail for a number of reasons.

Failures due to:

- telecommunications,
- hardware,
- software.

Whichever the cause of the failure, the user will expect that the system can be recovered quickly and that the applications are free from data corruption.

Inconsistencies within applications can result in:

- the user losing confidence in the system,
- lengthly investigation into the cause of failure,
- protected systems down time whilst the data sets are reconstructed from source documentation.

Therefore, one significant aspect of recovery is the time taken to reconstruct application data sets. The most straightforward method of recovering is to duplicate them by backup. The advantage of a backup is that recovery after failure is extremely fast.

In various sensitive applications, frequent auditing is recommended. As a minimum, a daily control report should be produced, reconciling balances on the opening and closing versions of data sets. This report should, also, show in detail the origins of all transactions processed during the reporting period.

With the number of computer applications continuing to grow and with a similar increase in the number of people using them, a new type of back-up service is needed. To meet the demand, a number of companies have introduced guides to their applications, which include catalogues on CD ROM. The catalogue, in fact, serves as a comprehensive system engineering tool.

Details on system applications, specifications and service requirements are made available to all users. If a user is not sure what documents are needed, he/she can start by looking at the full index.

Companies are even making available dedicated internal e-mail messages and Internet pages. The latter being interactive and intelligent. Newsletters are published, which keep the users informed of new product developments, interesting applications and other IT activities.

The widespread use of computers throughout business and the rapid growth of Internet connectivity means that computer security should concern all organisations.

However, it involves more topics than might be supposed. Ranging from the technicalities of protecting networks, teleworking and mobile systems, through the legalities of computer crime and corporate responsibility, to the politics of registering and protecting encryption keys.

Many companies are rightly concerned about security in the teleworking environment. Security for the teleworker starts at ground level; whereas home PC users do not normally activate the password facility on their computer, this is necessary for the teleworker to prevent accidental damage to data by children, family, or visitors.

Extremely sophisticated identification systems now exist that can read retina patterns, fingerprints and infra-red emissions from faces..

One simple measure to prevent unauthorised outsiders dialling into the system is to install dial-back modems. However, this security measure is easy to side-step. Likewise, calling-line identification, which permits the computer to identify the calling number and refuse access if it not recognised, can be bypassed by the experienced people.

Encryption is essential for the transmission of any material passing down the line. A simple method is to employ software which uses the same code at either end to encode and decode data. The next level is to impose a code of the day, using an encryption device card which is synchronised with a similar calculator card within the network.

The most complex form of encryption available is the digital signature. Each user, or teleworker, has a private key linked to a public key made available on an electronic noticeboard. The user encodes the message with the private key and the message can be decoded by anyone holding the allocated public key. However, any message encoded with the public key can be decoded only by the holder of the private key.

2.6   Software Considerations

Developing large systems require a range of software to achieve the overall systems objective. Depending upon the application and hardware types, this range of software at best could be totally packaged, or at worst may need to be completely written specially for the system.

Software in a project is like a jigsaw puzzle. Each piece fulfils a role and each piece must integrate with other pieces to make the complete system.

The basic types of software used are:

- applications software,
- conversational software,
- database management software,
- system development software,
- network software,
- system support software.

Applying hardware and software knowledge to system engineering and the development of systems enables System Architects to choose individual applications from a range of developers and bring these together into a single system that best meets the needs of the company and its tasks, transparently, sharing data. It also enables standard software, such as spreadsheets, word-processing, presentation packages and databases, to be linked to engineering software.

The flexibility this gives is far better for users than the traditional closed systems environment that forms the basis of many engineering software packages. However, to take advantage of this environment the system developers must totally restructure their approach to system building, a complex and daunting task.

2.7   Relational Database

There have been considerable advances in data management systems. These are no longer just about storing simple groups of data for the Accounting department. The secured and controlled access to databases include work-flow applications which ensure that information is sent to the appropriate person at the appropriate time. Also, introduced are the data configuration modules which take individual pieces of engineering information, such as drawings, models, test results, specifications and legal documentation.

The data storage of these applications enable the relationships between these information objects to be defined, manipulated and visualised. In practical terms they enable questions about changing and effect, or which suppliers meet deadlines. Information such as this, based on relational databases, can be answered in a fraction of the time traditional environments permit.

Not every company is large enough, or wants to undertake this complex process, but it may still want data management software. Several companies have launched lower-cost, object-orientated, but extremely powerful data management products that work within the PC and Windows environment.

While Windows has made the systems accessible to all, most of the products recently introduced into the knowledge-based environment, are software packages based on concepts that have been around for atleast ten years, with nothing more than a Windows-style interface. They do not exploit the new method of creating and utilising software and data that Windows and other operating systems offer. Two key elements to this, are the concept of data sharing between applications through 'object' technology and the dynamic linking of software such as packets, can be put together to create a single application suite specifically configured for a particular user.

Relational databases have now been around for some twenty years and have received much praise from system engineers who have seen their own productivity rate increase and systems easier to maintain and extend. Simultaneously, the end users are becoming proactive in deciding the appearance of their systems. They seek far greater control in customising their software.

To this effect, the users realise the simple fact that all computer systems need to store data and the simplest way to do so is to use flat files. The data are basically placed as a series of fields, grouped into records and stored sequentially on some magnetic media, usually tape or disk.

When writing logic to access these data the system engineer needed to understand where on the magnetic media the data were stored. This led to data and logic becoming inextricably linked, making it difficult to alter the system, should either change. Because of the way in which the data were stored, the developer often had to duplicate the storage of information, because different logic requirements needed different formats of data. Routines needed to access, update and delete information were not provided as standard routines and hence similar to access routines were frequently rewritten by various development teams.

Data could not be presented to the end user in an easily understandable format and the tools were very technical and demanded much training and computing expertise.

In answer to these problems, the first databases started to appear in the seventies. These were network and hierarchical types of database. In such systems the schema, or underlying data layout, had to follow strict rules such that it formed a hierarchy or network as the names suggest. The routines to access the data overcame some of the disadvantages of the flat file systems.

Currently, Data Warehousing is the term the technology organisations use to describe and to make sense of corporate data. It encompasses such diverse areas as Parallel Database Systems and Corporate Data Management.

Given the current advances in data acquisition and storage technologies, the problem of how to turn raw data into useful information is becoming ever more significant.

However, system developers using such systems have to understand fully the underlying and potentially complex data layout and navigate around the data structures very carefully to access the correct data.

The birth and growth of the newest type of database, the Relational Database Management System (RDBMS) changed the traditional way of storing data. The underlying data layout does not have to be contorted into any networks or hierarchies. Instead, the data mirror real life. Data are held in a series of tables, or data matrices and can contain any interrelationships which are required by the users. In short, relational databases give all the advantages of earlier database types, whilst remaining simple to use and design.

Another benefit of an RDBMS is that, instead of proprietary query languages, which are tied to one supplier's database, there is an industry standard query
language called Structured Query Language (SQL - sometimes pronounced sequel), which is used by the majority of relational databases. Also, a 4th Generation Language (4GL) environment is normally wrapped around the database to provide such facilities as end user report-writers and screen-painters for rapid screen development.

The RDBMS is, basically, a number of spreadsheets, or tables, related to each other by fields, or keys in each table. An in-house system, or package based on the RDBMS, will contain many standard screens and reports, but also gives the user the added advantage of accessing the database directly with the SQL.

One advantage of an RDBMS is the ease with which extra data requirements can be accommodated. Any reports, or screens, that had previously been written would be unaffected by any additions. There is generally no limit to the number of tables, the number of columns in the tables and the number of records. A distinct advantage of an RDBMS is that totally ad-hoc queries can be made quickly on any data.

Of course, some end users may not wish to understand the logical structure of the RDBMS. However, many users are computer literate and may wish to make use of the powerful facilities of the SQL and other tools available within the RDBMS. Some users may even wish to have their own particular 'views' of the database.

'User views' may offer more frequent access and user friendliness, but they still give complete control over which data a user accesses, right down to the field level. When a user view is created via the SQL, the user's sign-on identity will be included in the SQL. Additionally, sophisticated packages use the power of the database to create very powerful security features.

Many systems engineers will have experienced the situation of being forced to change a system application because the company's computer hardware changed. This is not so with the modern RDBMS. An RDBMS will run on a number of platforms. The system application will look identical on different hardware, from mainframes to PCs, hence protecting the organisation's investment in software and user/staff training.

Many relational databases are supplied with a data dictionary as a standard facility. These dictionaries hold details about the database and any application held therein. These data dictionaries encompass such areas as design specifications, program logic and data structures. They even extend this facility to allow users to define their own specifications and validations.

As the data dictionary contains so much information, it is a natural progression for a system application to be generated automatically. Already some systems allow the system engineer to specify requirements in a detailed, structured fashion and then speedily generate the application.

It is expected, imminently, that these data dictionaries to be front-ended to the users, for them to generate and change their applications, without any technical, or data processing skills.

2.8   Distributed Systems Processing

Shortly after the personal computer was introduced, businesses became enamoured with the idea of connecting groups of PCs together to share information and other resources.

The Windows 95, NT and their successors enable this and the integration of existing mainframe applications with PC users. With the right connectivity and the Client Server technology, the PC users will begin to see a major improvement in multi-tasking and in automating applications and PC functions.

Over the last few years Client Server technology has become a well used phrase in the Information Technology industry. Client Server extends the server functions with on a LAN (Local Area Network), such as data and printer sharing. It enables the workstation (the user) to perform tasks in a co-operative way with the server. This makes the most of the strengths of both, user and server.

The user can have a very easy to use Graphical User Interface (GUI), exploiting the power of the PC to display information and provide some localised processing. Meanwhile departmental and corporate information can be held on and shared by one or more servers of varying sizes.

The sheer computing power which is now available on a single user's desktop has led to demand for ever-increasing degrees of sophistication for the user environment.

A modern user demands applications supporting:

- windows,
- icons,
- mice,
- pull-down menus,
- inter-applications enquiries,
- inter-person communications,
- database access,
- on-line help system.

Ever since computers were able to store data in large quantities, the software people thought of processing methods and ways of working in parallel modes. The idea, originally, came across to programmers at the time when transistors started to make their impact on the increased memory available on the larger mainframes.

Although the memory was there, parallel processing came to its infancy with the advent of distributed processing. In the mid-sixties, different types of work could be stored and processed on a number of different medium-sized computers. One such distributed processor would be dealing with sales and the other with manufacturing and both would be sharing information from one common database. In a real-time application, the same medium-sized computer would be updating the files independently.

Machines such as the DEC's VAX systems, Gould's SCI-CLONE/32 and Sequent Balance 8000 SPP systems and others were able to support, on an average, ten visual display terminals and a dedicated local printer. Each distributed processor was capable of tackling its own system and simultaneously, in a parallel mode (by being networked), it passed the results and the processed data to another distributed processor, or to a number of mainframes.

Universities followed the commercial lead with ambitions that led them to today's impact of smaller processors and more capacity. The industrial financial backing and support enabled the academic sector to move into a new era, thus, once more taking the lead in computer processing. This lead would have not been possible, had it not been for the new programming languages emerging from the university researchers.

Capacity wise, industry was still restricted. The performance in all the technological devices, until very recently, was thought of being inferior, in comparison to the know-how available. Parallel processing was not possible, because the chip with high capacity and the right language to program it, just did not exist. Many manufacturers and many academics collaborated to reach such an ideal. Inmos was one such environment where it was hoped that they achieved both - the superchip and the language to go with it. Human nature as it is, did not allow for further delays. The researchers not only worked on the idea of superchips, but also on networking these chips.

At the moment, parallel processing is being promoted by many computer
manufacturers as an economic solution to the problem of long run-times inherent in many complex applications. Many computer systems may be configured as a collection of loosely, or tightly coupled processors, yet most do not support the concept of true parallel processing. It is, therefore, important to distinguish between multi-processing, or resilient computing (as in Cray systems) and parallel processing.

A multi-processing system utilises several processors connected together by some form of network, common bus structure, shared memory system, or a combination of these. At any instant in time, different progress may be running concurrently on different processors.

Andreas Sofroniou

There are many advantages to a multi-processor approach. Expensive peripherals, such as disc drives may be shared between all processors; some systems allow simple plug-in of processor boards, rather than complete chassis assemblies minimising floor space consumed; more users may be supported as processing power increases. The principal advantage is that system throughput may be increased as processors are added, provided that input/output, or memory capacity do not become limiting factors.

In the ideal case, if a user application takes ten hours to run on a single processor, it could be made to run in one hour on a ten-processor system. Obviously, explicit parallelisation of any kind means that the programmer must grasp the principles of parallel operation on the machine, as well as understanding his/her application. By means of parallel processing tools, a user may have four processors, each responsible for concurrently dealing with respective quarters of the array.

As parallelism stands now, it is still unsatisfactory. Probably, with the emergence of smaller chips - smaller processors, more capacity, more inputs/outputs, more processing speeds, unlimited numbers being networked; true parallel processing, or perhaps concurrency can be achieved.

In the meantime, other innovations and other technological breakthroughs, together, with psychological and biological advances, may yet (collaboratively) solve the stagnation of parallel processing.

It is agreed that these systems point the way to the future of systems developing, providing open, highly sophisticated, but easily configurable, application suites. Using these new architectures and the speed at which they can be developed in these environments, the expertise and the benefits offered
to users by these architectures could soon see companies strongly competing. Several major organisations world-wide already have committed themselves to these new architectures in distributed/parallel processing.

Parallel computers have been available for two decades. They offer a potentially much higher performance/cost ratio than conventional sequential computers. Yet, only a small fraction of computers in use are based on parallel technology. The parallel computers in commercial use, are mainly symmetric multi-processors systems in which parallelism is handled by the operating system scheduling independent tasks on different processors.

True parallel programs are rare, even on multi-processor systems. The main reason for this, is the difficulty in designing parallel software which can be architecture independent.

2.9   Personal Computing

Keeping up with computing technology is in itself almost a non-achievable task. The first comment most systems engineers make, is that technology is advancing because users are looking for these advances and not just for technology's sake. While many technologists express scepticism at the new techniques and tools on offer, there are companies in which successful implementation has led to significant business improvements. Consequently, they are continuously looking for the next areas of improvement.

The opportunities offered by Microsoft's Windows environment has not gone unnoticed by software developers. Windows is now standard on PCs and offers users a common interface to applications and resources. With the capabilities of PCs and work-stations becoming closely matched, engineering software developers have started to introduce applications normally associated with work-stations into this environment. Solid and assembly modelling are being introduced onto PC platforms.

Within this approach the terminals are placed into the user department and he/she enters the data. Any errors are immediately brought to the notice of the user, who can quickly respond and make any necessary corrections.

Modelling, as a tool on personal computers, provides a new way of undertaking system design, although is still viewed with scepticism by many system engineers. Yet there is a growing body of evidence that benefits of using such PC tools greatly outweighs the investment costs.

The improved quality of the information that such systems rapidly generate at the earliest stages of the design process enable better decisions to be made and errors reduced. Feeding these into downstream activities gives even greater benefits.

The specially designed computer devices with limited memory and storage facilities include internal modems to dial the Internet via a telephone line. This enables the exchange of e-mail and the use of conventional applications.

Data and documents created by users are stored on the network. This entails savings on the terminal and personal computer. This, some users maintain, may be the end of the use of conventional software such as Windows.

Computer companies such as Apple, Compaq, Phillips and the instigator of it all, the Oracle relational database experts, expect the design of the PC-like
device to last for years without becoming obsolete. Being a 'network computer' every time it is plugged in it will do the technical work for the user and whenever switched on the user will be accessing the latest version of applications.

2.10   Network

A network is a logical method of linking terminals to a computer. Today, because of the decentralised nature of most organisations, systems comprise terminals which are located away from the supporting computer. Most systems are supporting out-plant terminal equipment which is close to the computer as 400 meters and as distant as several hundred or several thousand kilometres.

One interesting aspect of system management that has seen increasing development, is the control of data between suppliers and customers. With many major organisations out-sourcing considerable amounts of systems development, they are recognising that suppliers need to become extensions of their own data management systems, connected via the latest telecommunications links.

Therefore, several companies have developed programs which request suppliers to use the same systems as they are using and which are directly connected to their own networks. This enables these organisations to extend the benefits of their technology throughout their whole systems environment and handle data flow in a dramatically more efficient manner than possible.

While compatible systems are seen as the only practical approach to data communication between supplier and customer, a new standard for transferring data between systems has become available from suppliers.

The supplier/customer communications systems are the first step in a networking revolution likely to occur in industry. The Internet, high-speed telecommunications links and video conferring will enable data to be communicated and discussed at speeds hitherto impossible, dramatically improving business efficiency.

When designing systems for this environment consideration must be given to the way data is transmitted between these out-plant locations.

The basic elements of a telecommunication network are:

- terminals, used in a network environment varying in speed and type, dependent upon the volume of traffic and the uniqueness of the application,
- transmission lines, which can be either simplex, half-duplex, or full duplex. Lines are, also, categorised by their transmission speeds, namely subvoice grade, voice band, or wide band,

- modems, which are required to translate digital signals used by computers and the analogue signals used on telecommunication lines.

Terminals used in a network environment vary in speed and type, dependent upon the volume of traffic and the uniqueness of the application.

The performance (and perhaps cost) of a network design can be improved by:

- sharing processing load, as in distributive processing and front end processing,

- sharing telecommunication facilities, thus taking away the network message handling from the host computer, allowing it to be dedicated to other processing,
- both.

2.11   Intranet

An Intranet is like a miniature Internet designed solely for the use of a company and its employees. It uses the same technology that built the World Wide Web,
but in the privacy of the organisation. A special network protocol called TCP/IP permits anyone on the company's network to access a set of documents which are stored on a dedicated computer called an Intranet Server. Hypertext links allow the user to 'surf' from one document to another.

An Intranet can put all of a company's information - from sales figures to the cafeteria lunch menu on one large, free-form database. Ideally, it captures and shares all the information in an organisation that was previously hoarded, or duplicated.

Intranet technology has all the benefits of the Internet; it is easy to jump from document to document, or to find a piece of information on a particular subject, or to access data quickly from any computer. But it does not have the Internet's disadvantages. Intranet use a network connection to data rather than the Internet's telephone-based connection, so they respond more quickly. The users control the information on an intranet, so they know that it is relevant. Because it exists behind the security screen of the company's computer network, known as the 'firewall', an intranet is as safe from hackers as the network itself.

Installing an intranet is cheap enough to make it easily affordable for small businesses, provided they use a local area network (LAN). In addition to the LAN, a company needs to install TCP/IP and a Web browser. The hardware cost involved is that of buying a dedicated computer to act as the storage point for all the intranet pages.

The key to a successful intranet lies in gaining the co-operation of its users who have to keep the information up-to-date and relevant. That means not only installing a culture of 'information sharing', but also managing the process of updating that information. Maintaining an intranet is more of a management task than a technical one.

Training is another area that requires careful planning, even though the browser software is relatively easy to use. Few companies attempt formal training programmes.

While the first stage of an intranet project can be no more dramatic than inputting a telephone book, an increasing number of firms are using intranet access to organise their structured information. This can be sales trends, or reports and financial information, automatically extracted from a company's database and placed on an intranet page. The software required to build these systems is more complex, because unless it updates automatically, the data quickly becomes useless.

A technology that can make the intranet useful, is likely to be what the industry calls 'push' technology. Push technology has conquered the problem of information overload on the Internet. Instead of going out and gathering information, the user can tell the software what he/she is looking for and it delivers the relevant data, automatically.

Push technology works just as well on intranet. Instead of searching the entire intranet for information, users can set their browser to find it by using a keyword, or other related data.

2.12   Teleworking

Advances in communications induce the IT department to rethink the way their staff conduct their business. New technology effectively deployed, permits the management of information systems to respond to the constant pressure to reduce costs while at the same time continuing to improve service to user departments.

For many organisations, the workplace itself is being transformed. In such an increasingly competitive business environment, a key success factor is the ability to access, collect, process, distribute and act upon information rapidly from anywhere in the world. New ways of working, such as teleworking, have made the workplace and source of information virtually location independent and are revolutionising the speed, cost and flexibility of the workforce.

Andreas Sofroniou

A few years ago, teleworking meant staying at home occasionally to write a report and keeping in touch by telephone, or fax. Today, inexpensive and reliable communications solutions have transformed teleworking into a fast growing working practice that can bring substantial benefits to the IT department and its employees alike.

For systems development, the benefits include reduced overheads and improved productivity through using the time of key workers more efficiently and flexibly. For systems engineers it can mean greater control over their working environment and less stress. Advances in technology are enabling IT staff to do more for less. They can produce more systems and services of higher quality and with better user focus for less cost and with fewer people.

System engineers have eagerly invented labels for terms such as re-engineering, downsizing and outsourcing. But such jargon describes a genuine revolution in the systems environment. The latest buzzword, teleworking, refers to an equally substantive and growing method of work, namely, the ability (created by modern computing and telecommunications technology) of systems engineers to work when and where they can do so, most efficiently and effectively.

The challenges and the opportunities in both, the nature and location of work are particularly apparent. System engineers have more choice of where, when, how, with whom and for whom to work, than any generation in computing. System engineers can reach from almost any point, in seconds (by telephone, fax, or electronic mail) users and colleagues.

Faced with demanding users and intense competition from software houses, few IT departments can take success, or indeed survival, for granted. Constant renewal, regeneration and re-skilling are required.

Systems teams are re-engineering in the search for improvements in performance which will enable them to leap ahead, rather than merely catch up. They are aiming to reduce dependency upon fixed costs and particular locations, and are de-layering and slimming down in the search for greater efficiency, flexibility and responsiveness. By focusing upon core capabilities and key competencies, they are identifying areas of activity that can be outsourced, contracted out rather than performed by internal teams.

The relationships between people, information and tasks are also being reassessed critically and fundamentally. There are many ways in which IT departments can secure access to the skills they need. Work can be undertaken on a full or part-time basis, as a system engineer or contractor, for single or multiple projects, on a temporary or permanent basis. Teleworking represents a new way of working. A telecommunications link is used to secure access to people and information, and/or to interact with others.
The European Commission initiated a wide-ranging programme aimed at examining various aspects of teleworking. One such investigation is the COBRA (Constraints and Opportunities in Business Restructuring - an Analysis) project. A pan-European investigation of business restructuring by such means as delayering and re-engineering and the part played by teleworking.

For all the sophistication of available teleworking hardware, research shows that the telephone is still the most important device. The telephone has changed little in the last few years, atleast in terms of hardware. True, the cordless made an impact, but it still has its limitations. It has no real implications for teleworkers.

Where there have been significant developments is in the way calls are made and received. Many of the changes have been prompted by teleworking, particularly by the need to retain a seamless flow of communication between the home and other colleagues at the office.

While the telephone remains the pivotal teleworking device, it is almost impossible for most home-based workers to imagine life without the fax. With the ability to transmit documents and simple visuals in seconds its benefit is blindingly obvious.

Of course, the fax need not be a machine at all. It can be just a piece of software on a computer. In fact, more and more teleworkers send and receive all fax transmissions via their PCs. They do so with the addition of a modem. This device plugs into the PC to convert the computer's digital information into an analogue signal which can travel down telephone lines. It does the reverse for incoming faxes so that transmissions can be called up on screen instead of on a piece of fax paper.

Andreas Sofroniou

The fax modem saves a great deal of time. Instead of printing out a document, loading it into the machine and dialling the number, the modem user simply keys in the fax number, clicks on send and gets on with his or her next job. The recipient downloads a 'living' document ready for editing without the need to re-type.

Like all the other hardware, modems are getting smaller, cheaper and faster. Most external models, which plug into the PC and have their own power supply, are no bigger than a pocket size radio.

The internal modem is the size of a credit card and fits into a slot found on most PCs and even laptops. When the internal modem is attached to a suitably equipped mobile phone, it gives the teleworker true mobility.

Many users already have e-mail facilities on their personal computers. Every e-mail user is given a personal address by the Internet access service, or work organisation and they send and receive messages using their computer and modem. Software makes it easy to do this. To send, simply key in a message, select an address and click on the appropriate icon. To call up a message just click on 'read' and everyone is displayed instantly.

E-mail is catching on fast because it is quicker and less cumbersome than the fax and cheaper. Messages are sent by the organisations to which the users belong so every e-mail (even one to an address on the other side of the world) is a local call.

The best way for the PC-using teleworker to be kept within the fold of his/her organisation is to be networked. Most companies already network the computers in their office so that every worker is hooked up to one printer and

has shared access to information held on the master computer or server. It does not take much to expand this local area network (LAN) to a wide area network (WAN) so that remote workers have the same access.

The foundations of teleworking have already been laid, so it looks as if future changes will be incremental rather than revolutionary. The biggest development may well be a new kind of telephone line called ISDN (Integrated Services Digital Network). Because it is digital, ISDN allows huge amounts of data to flow between callers. It means that graphics and video (data-heavy for normal telephone lines to handle) can be transferred between teleworkers.

The applications are boundless. A home-based system engineer could remedy a system fault in another country. System architects could work on computer-aided tools together while hundreds of miles apart.

3: Object Oriented Methodology

3.1 Object Oriented System Development

Object-based technology is emerging as a development method that can lead to convergence between business processes and Information Technology systems, with some substantial benefits. An object in business or system terms has inputs, processes and outputs. Breaking complex business processes into identifiable, discrete objects is the first stage of business re-engineering, or process re-design.

Creating a matching object on the computer system (some call it 'fabrication') then linking them together (assembly) means that the system process should then mirror the business process. Subsequently, changes and improvements to a business process should be able to be matched quickly by an update to the corresponding system object.

Where common objects are used many times, this can lead to substantial savings of time and cost. Common objects are now becoming commercially available, to be incorporated into applications, rather like clipart and drawings are available for documents.

The idea of designing a system the data-driven way is probably best served by the Object Oriented Methodology (OOM). As a method for system development OOM allows the delivery of solutions to users' problems and requirements as close as possible to the real way the commercial world works. It assists the system engineers to represent and closely match the business functions.

It is claimed that OOM shortens the development lifecycle and that the system developed offers longer term benefits, less post-implementational costs, flexibility in building and reusability of the models created.

It is true to say that the terminology of OOM differs from that of the established methodologies, such as SSADM. It can be demonstrated though, that an object model can be considered as an entity model. Probably the most frequently cited model is that of the entity relationship model, where the 'real world' is represented in terms of entities, the relationship between entities and the attributes associated with entities.

Entities represent objects of interest, such as 'employees', 'department' and 'project'. Relationships represent named associations between entities. A department employs many employees. An employee is assigned to a number of projects. 'Employs' and 'is assigned to' are both relationships in the entity-relationship approach. Attributes are properties of an entity or relationship. 'Name' is an attribute of the entity 'employee'.

Associations is a form of abstraction in which instances of one entity are associated with instances of another entity. Association is implicit in the way relationships on entity models are defined.

The major difference between entities and objects is:

- An entity model gives a useful framework for painting the structured detail of a database system.
- Objects have more ambitious a purpose. An object is designed
  to encapsulate both, a structured and behavioural aspect.

Therefore, an object model gives a means for designing not only a database structure, but also shows how that database structure is to be used. An object models files and it also models constraints and transactions.

The easiest way to build an object model is to exploit some of the inherent strengths of entity modelling and extend them with some structural and behavioural abstractions.

3.2 Object Oriented Lifecycle

A typical lifecycle for the development of object oriented systems modelling consists of six stages, where all steps are fully defined.

Andreas Sofroniou

These missions (stages) are:

- strategic modelling,
- analysis modelling,
- design modelling,
- implementation modelling,
- construction,
- delivery.

Each mission (stage) may be met by the introduction of new processes to meet objectives, or developing systems to support and supplement existing business processes. This type of strategic modelling maps directly to the domain decomposition used in analysis and design and is known as Business Re-engineering

3.3   Analysis And Design Modelling

The typical analysis and design for object orientation involves a number of stages:

- domain decomposition,
- static modelling,
- dynamic modelling.

In the domain decomposition, the identification of layers is a method of decomposing the problem domain. For example, a system representing a company may have layers for:

- marketing,
- sales,
- accounts,
- production.

The diagram below represents the problem domain, including its constituents parts of Processing Hospital Patient:

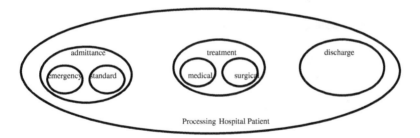

Static and dynamic models can now be created for the domain (or domains) of interest as defined by a domain diagram. Static object models of a sub-domain will generally be adequate to support all the business objects of interest with the particular domain.

Dynamic models will be unique at the higher level, but reusable events/objects may occur within the lower level system dynamic, hence some reusability.

Andreas Sofroniou

The static model is represented by Entity Type Diagrams. The static modelling keys are:

- object, represented by a rectangle,

- message flow, shown as an unidirectional arrow,

- bi-directional message flow,

- classification inheritance,

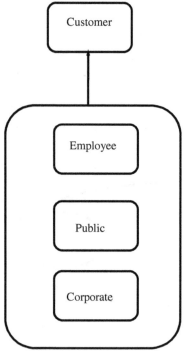

The dynamic aspects of a system can be modelled using another technique. These are known as Event Type Diagrams and as such represent the global finite state machine that gives instance to the inert or static objects as defined in the static model.

The components of the dynamic object model are:

- event:

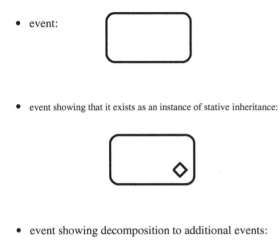

- event showing that it exists as an instance of stative inheritance:

- event showing decomposition to additional events:

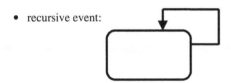

- recursive event:

- event sequence:

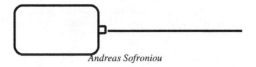

- compulsory and sequence:

Andreas Sofroniou

Events give rise to methods that support their existence. These methods are implemented by a series of rules. Instead of imbedding the rules within the body of a particular algorithm, these rules are defined in a set of methods that are attached to the relevant objects.

Rules may represent:

- business policy,
- regulations,
- triggers,
- exceptions,
- declarative descriptions of operations,
- control regimes.

Rules and Assertions:

- rules capture second order information about objects,
- rules can capture system control regimes,
- rules may be converted to assertions and class invariant at design time.

Assertions are:

- pre-conditions,
- post-conditions,
- invariance-conditions.

The deliverables from the analysis and design phase are:

- domain decomposition,
- static modelling (Entity Type Diagrams),
- dynamic modelling (Event Type Diagrams).

These are then taken forward to the implementation modelling phase.

The production of the method using a more formal and rigorous approach comes during the implementation modelling phase and requires all methods to be specified.

The generation of implementation specification methods must be performed in two directions. From the major events downwards through the atomic events and from the objects and sub-atomic events, so that the objects are mapped to the events and adhere to encapsulation.

3.4   Construction And Reuse

There are many different ways in which to build object oriented systems. These approaches fall into distinct groups. These major groups are formed due to the nature of programming languages and tools available:

- Hand carving, requiring large teams over extended periods of time. The languages that fall into this category are 3GLs and 4GLs. Both of these languages do not support inheritance of any kind, therefore, additional work is required.
- Semi-automated, relies on the use of languages that are fully compliant with the requirements of an object oriented environment in that they support all construct required for semantic modelling. The languages can be enhanced 3GLs and Object Oriented Database Management Systems (OODMS).

- Automated approach, makes use of CASE (Computer-aided Software Engineering) tools. These tool sets enable support for the semantic modelling deliverables of static and dynamic models. This approach, also, generates code, requiring minimal human intervention.

3.5   Rapid Business Modelling

The object oriented technology offers models that are intrinsically richer in their semantic content and therefore smaller and more easily digestible. The benefits of rapid modelling can be capitalised by using these models as a living requirements catalogue. The requirements catalogue becomes a much smaller textual document covering the area of strategic platforms and tools. Thus, the system functionality is described by a model and not text.

The true power of object technology can be seen in a model generated to capture and build the system for the IT and non-IT people. The rapid business modelling approach utilises the strength of the semantic modelling approach as a requirements catalogue is no longer a purely textual document.

Strategic requirements are entered into the requirements catalogue that describe:

- hardware,
- platform,
- operating systems,
- programming languages,
- tool set,
- volumetric,
- top level business area,
- critical business processes.

The in-depth functional requirements of the system are encapsulated within the object model that is now made part of the requirements catalogue. The object model acts as the design and the requirement. The object model is even more important in the rapid lifecycle approach.

An even bigger saving in terms of analysis and design can be made by using relational models that may already exist (based on structured methods). These existing models can be converted to an object oriented model (both static and dynamic) very rapidly that can encapsulate all the richness of the original model. The value of this approach is in maximising the original investment made in developing the model and speed taken to produce it.

If no existing relational structured model, or system exists, this approach must use the standard business modelling techniques to produce the first cut and subsequent refined object model. However, the conversion method is fully described below.

The conversion method is broken down into three main activities:

- identify the major objects,
- perform object identification,
- methods statement.

Each object (entity) shown on the main Entity Type Diagram must be further refined to show a greater level of class detail. However, to stop the model from becoming difficult to navigate, produce an Entity Type Diagram for every entity identified on the main Entity Type Diagram.

The general approach to produce an event model from a relational model is to review the appropriate dataflow diagram to find that dataflows across the boundaries to the processes that are of business interest. The Structured English that describes the processes of interest, will describe these events in much more detail than that shown on the process model (dataflow diagrams) as this model constitutes the full event model to a level of great detail.

The Human Computer Interface (HCI) consisting of screens, forms and letters is also of value to elicit the events occurring in a process, as these interactions points are the triggers for the event having occurred.

Andreas Sofroniou

3.6   Benefits And Disadvantages

Object oriented technologies promise a number of significant benefits. It will lead to larger scale systems that organise information more effectively and adapt more easily to changing needs.

Possible benefits include:

- Faster production. The speed advantage comes from the reuse of existing objects, all the design work of the existing model of the processes and all the formal procedures that are bypassed by rapid prototyping.

- Higher quality. The increase in quality stems from the fact that programs are assembled out of existing proven components rather than being written from scratch. Also, the modularisation of object orientation reduces the interaction among components of a program, making it easier to verify functionality.

- Easier maintenance. Object oriented technology can reduce maintenance because it produces higher quality systems in the first instance. If errors occur, these can be easily located, because of the natural mapping between the structure of the software and the real world it models. Once located, the errors are generally confined to a small area of the problem, typically an object, so the effect of making a change has little or no effect on the rest of the system.

3.7   Experience-based OOM

Every analysis and design methodology gives directions on how to solve a problem and how to include the user requirements into an effective system and user accepted tool. Almost every method explains how to break up a problem, into two basic components: data structure and processes.

Simply stated, the OOM revolutionises the development of applications for personal computers. 4th generation application development products allow the Analyst to utilise the object oriented analysis and design (OOA/OOD) approach to computer application development.

The details of the OOM are brought to life by such readily available products, facilitating a visual, user friendly extension of OO programming design and implementation concepts. The use of Classes, Subclasses, Inheritance, Encapsulation and Polymorphism are an inherent part of such application development packages.

The OOM approach provides one of the important means with which to meet the pressures on the commercial systems function and to integrate IT with business objectives.

OOM concepts have been implemented in:

- programming languages,
- analysis and design methods,
- database management systems,
- operating systems,
- application development environments.

The basic conceptual elements of the object model are simple. Everything is treated as an object. Objects communicate by passing messages. A number of advantages accrue from the OOM approach with respect to software programming and systems development, in general.

A user and an Analyst can have a meaningful discussion on a given object, even though each will have a different view of the object. The user will be concerned with what it does, the Analyst with how it does it. This is in contrast to the traditional methods where the user's problems and requirements, their solutions and their incorporation in the design, involves distinct representation at each stage. Such that users and Analysts speak different languages in respect to the same problem.

Relating to the above, the OOM offers a set of clear conceptual and technical advantages which may go some significant way towards addressing most of the difficulties faced in developing a required system.

The computer languages (evolutionary) are divided into four generations:

1GL: includes the binary languages, sequences of the bits,
2GL: includes the assemblers,
3GL: high level languages, COBOL, PL/1,
4GL: The self-generating code languages,
5GL: The artificial intelligence, the non-procedural languages.

The OOM enthusiast place the non-procedural languages under 4GL and claim that the OO languages and methodology are the primary representative of 5GL.

The main fact remains, that the use of object oriented applications development is currently increasing and will influence the decisions regarding systems development, implementation strategies and software tool deployment during the remainder of this decade.

4: Structured Systems Analysis And Design

4.1   The Background Of Structured Analysis

As a background to structured methodology, it is worth mentioning that it all started with IBM and the problems this giant of computing was facing with the programming problems. IBM called in psychologist Larry Constantine who, as the story goes, diagnosed that the programmers were projecting their own individual perceptions of how the specifications were written.

Larry Constantine's write-up on a structured method included ideas from his psycho-physiological studies and terms such as afferent and efferent. His suggestions worked for IBM and soon after, others followed with variations. Names such as Gane and Sarson, Yourdon, James Martin and other gurus, who again were followed by BIS Modus, LBMS-LSDM and with CCTA the SSADM and many, many more familiar names.

The differences among the protagonists were not of any consequence. Gane and Sarson used to say that all details could be gather within a diagram and then modularise into smaller sections within boundaries. Yourdon maintained that anything bigger than an A4 paper was too complicated. Now-a-days, everybody is recommending five boxes on an average within a boundary, maximum seven and three the minimum. Any more than seven boxes and the analyst will take into consideration the possibility of decomposing to a lower level.

The point is that, instead of just picking up the keyboard of the dummy terminal and starting to program, everybody in the commercial world is now following a structured method. Whether the systems designed are successful or not, depends on the training and experience the systems engineers bear with them. In a similar way this is what the contents of this book are trying to assimilate.

4.2   The Need For Structured Analysis And Design

Systems Analysis consists of an evolving set of tools and techniques which have grown out of the success of structured designing. The underlying concept is the building of a logical model, a non-physical system, using a diagrammatic representation which enables the users and analysts to get a clear and common understanding of the required system. How its parts fit together and how it answers to the users' needs.

Since Computer-aided Software Engineering (CASE) tools are used to build a logical model, structured methodology involves building a system by successive refinement by:

- producing an overall system dataflow diagram (DFD),
- developing detailed dataflows,
- defining the detail of data structure and process logic,

The whole of the analysis and designing of the system is done by:

- analysing top-down,
- designing top-down,
- developing top-down,
- testing top-down.

It is recognised that good development involves iteration and an Analyst has to be prepared to refine the logical model and the physical design in the light of information resulting from the use of an early version of that model, or design. This may involve some reverse engineering of the processes of an earlier physical system, or an earlier version of the analysis exercise.

In many ways, systems analysis and designing is the toughest part of the development of an information technology system. The problems encountered by an Analyst in a company environment will include the:

- technical difficulty of the work,
- demand of knowledge of current technology,

- political difficulties that arise,
- several conflicting interest user groups,
- communication difficulties among people of different backgrounds,
- different views, requirements and priorities.

It is the compounding of these difficulties that makes systems analysis so demanding. The fact that the Analyst becomes the middleman between user groups and has the intuitive approach for the users' problems and their solutions. The Analyst must bring forward what is currently possible in an onrushing technology and what is optimum for the business run by people. Making the match in a way which is acceptable to all.

Even with the best CASE tool, no methodology will enable the Analyst to know what is in a user's mind and has no way of showing a tangible model of the system, apart from the diagrams of the logical phases and their short descriptions. On the other hand, it is hard for the users to imagine what the new system is going to do for them, until it is actually up and running, by which time it may be too late to perform any costly post-implementational repairs and additions.

To begin with, in order to ease the communication with the users, an Analyst can use the tools of structured systems analysis to prepare a functional specification which:

- is comprehended and agreed by the users,
- sets out the logical requirements of the system without dictating a physical implementation,
- expresses preferences and trade-offs.

The building of a logical model, which clearly communicates to users what the systems will and will not do, is crucially important. The users cannot afford to wait until the system is operational, before they see what they get. The analysing and designing of the logical phases are, therefore, of paramount importance in telling the users what to expect.

4.3   Tools For Analysis

At a general level, it can be said that just like an existing system, the new system will represent (for example) the processing of orders from customers, the orders will be checked against a file of products available, check on a file holding a customer's details and then dispatch the goods with an invoice.

This can be shown in a logical DFD:

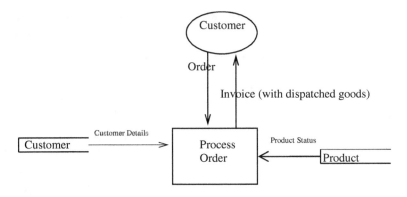

In this DFD four symbols were used:

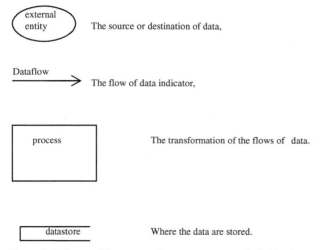

The source or destination of data,

The flow of data indicator,

The transformation of the flows of data.

Where the data are stored.

The symbols above and the concepts they represent, are at a logical level:

- An external entity may represent a client/customer, or another entity/department from within an organisation.
- A flow of data may physically be contained in a letter, or an invoice; anywhere data pass from one entity or process to another.
- A process may physically be a clerk calculating charges, or a combination of manual and automated activities.
- A datastore can be a card file, a filing cabinet, or a file on a tape or disk.

Using the four symbols enables the Analyst to draw a diagram of the system without committing the system as to how it will be implemented.

The example of 'Process Order' can be expanded to show the logical functions within the present system. The checking of incoming orders can be shown. Once the orders have been validated, a supplier can be found who is willing to give discounts on large orders.

The DFD that follows shows the checking of each order and in return the assembling of bulk orders to the supplier, to benefit from a discount. In this DFD a boundary has been introduced to separate the external entities from the activities relating to the 'handling of orders'. In a way the boundary signifies the modularisation of the processes in the functions relating to 'verifying and assembling of orders' (within the 'handling'), the data flowing to and from various 'boxes' and the storing of the data in the datastores.

The example shown, is of course a summary of a lot of details regarding orders. Normally, the average of five boxes are shown within a boundary and further details are always shown in the exploded, lower level of the DFD. If necessary, each component process box can itself be broken down to a third level of detail.

Within the boundaries of the top level and the subsequent exploded second and third levels, other processes will be introduced. In elaborating the example of 'orders', processes such as 'invoicing', 'accounts receivable', 'assign shipment' etc. will be introduced.

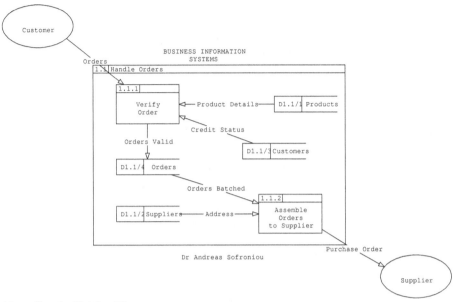

Dr Andreas Sofroniou

4.4 Drawing Dataflow Diagrams

The idea of a chart for representing the flow of data through a system is not new. In analysing, as it was previously shown, symbols are needed together with their descriptions.

Herewith each symbol and its conventions are examined in detail:

External entities are the logical classes of things, or people which represent a source/recipient of transactions, such as Customers, Employees, Suppliers, Taxpayers, Policy Holders. They may, also, be a source or destination within an organisation; Accounts Department, Warehouse, Factory. Where the system accepts data from another system, or returns data to it, that other system is an external entity.

The External Entity can be identified by a lower-case letter in the upper left-hand corner for reference.

To avoid crossing dataflow lines, the same entity can be drawn more than once on the same diagram; two or more boxes per entity can be identified by an angled line in the bottom right-hand corner, thus:

By designating a thing or a system as an external entity, it is implicitly stated that it is outside the boundary of the system being considered.

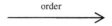

The dataflow is symbolised by an arrow, with an arrowhead showing the direction of the flow. In the top level of a diagram, a double-headed arrow may be used in place of two arrows.

Each dataflow is a 'pipe' which is used for data to be sent. Each 'pipe' has a meaningful description of the contents written alongside it. The description of the dataflow will include the attributes, as early in the design as possible.

The Analyst needs to describe the function of each process and give each process a unique numerical identifier. Each time the process is exploded so is the number. For instance, the number of the process in the upper-most level is 1, where as the exploded process will have its boxes numbered 1.1, 1.2, 1.3 etc. At the lower level the process numbered 1.1, will now be numbered 1.1.1 and so on and so forth.

The description of the function should be an imperative sentence, ideally consisting of an active verb:

* Verify,
* Assemble,
* Compute,
* Extract.

followed by an object or object clause:

* Extract - monthly sales,
* Enter - customer details.
* Verify - stock availability.

Without a physical commitment, during analysis there are places where data are defined and stored between processes.

Datastores can be symbolised by a pair of horizontal lines, closed at one end. Each datastore can be identified by the letter 'D' and a number, in a box at the left-hand side.

D1	Customer

The name should be chosen to be most descriptive to the user.

To avoid complicating a dataflow diagram with crossed lines, the same datastore can be drawn more than once on the same diagram, identifying duplicate datastores by an additional vertical line at the left.

	D1	Customer

4.5   Explosion Conventions

Each process in the top level DFD can be exploded to become a lower level DFD. Each process at the lower level will need to be related back to the higher level process, by giving the lower level process box an identification number which is a decimal of the high-level process. Thus, box number 2 is decomposed into 2.1, 2.2, 2.3, 2.4, 2.5. Should it be necessary to go to a third level, 2.5 is decomposed into 2.5.1, 2.5.2, 2.5.3, 2.5.4, 2.5.5.

The lower level DFD is drawn within the boundary which represents the higher level process. All dataflows in and out of the higher level process must enter and leave the boundary. Datastores which are shown inside the boundary of the upper level, at the lower level DFD are shown outside the boundary.

Once the DFDs have been drawn and described, the Analyst has to decide whether a function should remain in the level shown, or identify lower level functions which are additions to the ones shown on the higher level processes.

To summarise the diagrammatic representation of an existing, or required system, identify the:

- External Entity. This involves a preliminary system boundary. Place the external entities outside the boundary, with dataflows into and out of the boundary, thus connecting the external entities with the processes inside the boundary.
- Inputs and the outputs (those arrows which represent the dataflows). What one expects in the normal course of any business. As the amount of dataflows increases invent logical groupings of inputs and outputs.
- Processes which represent the functions within the DFD boundary. The Analyst must remember that a process is triggered by a dataflow, the input of data which require a function. Once the process has undergone the transaction, the details are flowed out to be stored.
- Datastore, which can be the representative of a cupboard, a drawer, or a current system. The input of the data into a datastore can be on a temporary, or permanent basis. Whatever goes into a datastore must come out, otherwise the datastore will be the dead end of the information cycle.

4.6   Using The Methodology

As computers get cheaper, many companies are finding that they can gain from operating systems. Additionally, many organisation find the benefit of using structured methodologies for the development of new systems. Structured analysis is useful in investigating the existing systems, be it manual or automated. The structured methods help with the understanding of the problems faced by a business and the obstacles in running a profitable environment.

Structured analysis definitely helps in deciding whether to install a computer and what parts of the systems to develop and interface the automated system with manual systems, clerical procedures other systems and perhaps suppliers' systems - customer companies' systems.
To answer such questions, maybe an initial study will assist in making a decision. Most certainly the answers will be focused on the questions of:

- What is wrong with the current situation?
- What improvements are possible?
- What are the benefits?
- Who will be affected by the new system?

In an organisation of any size, there is usually a stream of requirements from user departments for improvements in information technology services. While some of these requests can be met by improving the current systems, such as better response time, some may still bear further enhancements of the existing operating systems.

Many companies prefer to start from scratch and develop new systems and bring new ideas in running their computer systems. In such cases, the development of new systems is overdone. Many organisations find that the demand for new systems is several times greater than the resources allow.

An initial study (lasting from two days to a couple of weeks), will help to decide the route to be followed. The Analyst should study the requests and meet with the managers to get the background and to begin to assess the costs and benefits of a possible new system.

It is useful to investigate the reasons for wanting to build a new system. It is fair to the analyst to remember that a new system may offer the opportunity to:

- increase revenue,
- avoid costs,
- improve service.

By the end of the initial study, the Analyst should be confident about the costs and the benefits resulting from a proposed system. The outcome of the initial study will be reviewed by the appropriate level of management or steering users group.

Once the go-ahead is authorised, a detailed study can begin. The detailed study builds on facts, current policies, functions and methods of transacting a business. The activities of the detailed study will include:

- who the users of a new system will be,
- the functional areas considered,
- collect views of objectives and preferences.

At this stage the building of a logical model of the current system starts and together with the refined estimates, a statement of possible increased revenue, avoidable costs and improved services will be included in the detailed study.

As a result of this phase of the study, reviews will follow and a decision is usually made to continue the project to the next set of steps.

The definition of alternative should follow. Until the advent of structured methods, the offering of a 'menu' has not been a practical proposition, because the presentation of alternatives to users has been difficult. With structured analysis and designing, the presentation of alternative solutions involves the users in making a business decision and offers the system as an answer to what the user community requires.

The activities involved in the development of alternatives include:

- deriving objectives from the current systems,
- cataloguing of the new requirements,
- developing a logical model of the new system,

Typically, the logical model by this stage consists of the overall DFD and the logical data structure. This logical model will be reviewed in detail with users and any feedback will be used to alter the documentation accordingly and will be incorporated in the design of the phase.

The analyst frequently acts as agent for the users in these phases, just like an architect will supervise the construction of a building, ensuring that the plans are being followed. The Analyst will keep the logical model up-to-date, through design and implementation, especially the DFDs (dataflow diagrams).

4.7 Bringing Structured Analysis To Companies

There are various steps which need to be taken in order to introduce the structured techniques into a systems development organisation, with consideration to the benefits expected, together with the problems that people experienced in using systems.

The main steps involved in implementing a structured methodology in a company, are:

1. Reviewing the method used for projects.

   The amount of work involved in assessing the procedures used in systems development will vary greatly, depending on whether a formal structured methodology has been adopted, or whether the organisation has created its own ground rules.

Any method based on structured analysis will specify a sequence of activities to be followed in creating a system, the products to be developed at each stage and the management controls to be applied. Almost any established method will, in general, specify the conduct of a feasibility study. Following a feasibility study, a detailed design, followed by coding and testing.

If such a methodology is already used, check that:

- it does not encourage pre-mature physical design. If so ensure that this is modified to allow for the logical stages to be introduced prior to entering the physical stage.
- The methodology in existence does not subscribe to over-documentation - the exhaustive narrative details. The DFDs and data modelling can easily replace the excessive writing and descriptions.
- The present method allows for top-down development. This point raises a more fundamental issue. That of the 'straight-line-approach'. Many systems engineers assume that a well-managed development project goes in a 'straight line', from the feasibility study to the analysis, through design into testing and users acceptance. The path of such a project can be completed by using a 'spiral' approach.

The spiral concept reflects the reality of the problems faced in systems development. At each progressing phase a skeleton is built, this is then logicalised and walked through to see how well the logical phases work and then reverse to put more details into the study. Thus, the project control needs to accommodate the delivery of sensible products; dataflow diagrams, data structures and functional analysis, rather than the completion of activities.

2. Establish standards for the use of a CASE (Computer-aided Software Engineering) tool.

A decision may have to be made to acquire a CASE tool. This is a good support for the Analyst's responsibilities in diagramming the system-to-be. It is very convenient to have a tool for diagrammatic representations for the maintenance and easy updating of diagrams and specifications in general.

CASE tools are progressing so quickly, the latest versions include the facilities for quick prototyping and transforming the descriptions to structured English and in turn to 4GLs, coding.

3. The tools and techniques of structured systems analysis must be as simple and as realistic as possible. To use any system engineering techniques expertly needs experience; study and practice. While the rules and conventions can be learnt easily, the hardest thing appears to be at the logical level.

Whatever the difficulty, a DFD showing sequence of events improves the understanding of the users and the analyst's tasks become much easier. In analysis and design users are asked to think about problems at a higher level of abstraction and this can take time and persistence.

Apart from the fluency with the logical tools, the analysts need to become familiar with the emerging support software. If the ground rules for projects are to change, analysts will have to explain them to the users. Analysts need to be briefed on new methodology and think through its implications for users.

If structured development is to be used, the Analysts must be thoroughly briefed on the concept and the implementation plan of each project with which they are concerned. The Analyst, most certainly, must be able to criticise a design in the light of the structured methodology principles.

4. As the new structured techniques and approaches improve communication with users and involve them more in setting the direction of the project, they are welcomed by the user community. At the same time, the new ideas represent a change in the rules of developing systems, in a positive way, as the implications and benefits are clearly explained in the process of designing.

The communication with the users, as each 'structured' project starts, should cover the following points:

- the notation of the DFD,
- the concept of presenting a 'menu' of alternative systems for the users to consider,

- the briefing on the structured method,
- a warning on the participation and involvement required on the part of the users,
- reassurance that the new method for system development does not impose more effort,
- that the project will not generate more paperwork for the users.

In some companies, the users are trained to draw their own DFDs and their own descriptions in structured English. The Analyst ought to encourage this, provided the individual user wants to go ahead with this. This concept, in many organisations, proved very beneficial, in as much as the communication difficulties experienced prior to this method, they just disappeared. The users felt as if they were guiding the project the way it suited them.

Where specific executives are assigned as members of the Users Committee, it is desirable that they should be trained in structure methodology. This will give them the ability to present the business, their point of view and the requirements, and define them to the Analyst. The Executives trained in structured analysis can be more informed critics of the logical models produced by the system engineering area.

With structured training, the users will be able to quantify most of the benefits that result from improved productivity and the better management time and resources.

The benefits from using structured systems analysis, from the system engineering point of view, are even more profound:

- users get a much more vivid idea of the proposed system from logical DFDs, than they do from narratives and excessive descriptions,
- presenting the system in terms of logical DFD reduces the misunderstandings and issues,
- the interfaces between the new system and existing systems are shown clearly by the DFD and the data model,
- the use of logical models eliminates duplications,

The benefits, of course, are not free from potential problems. The problems may be partly due to the change in working procedures and partly the result of the discipline imposed by the logical phases. This type of problem can easily be reduced by:

- introducing training to the users and the analysts as early in the project as possible,
- the effort and degree of detail required, especially in building the data model is often resisted. The consolation here is that, if the data are right in the first attempt, then less effort will be needed in the latter stages of development,
- where structured English are introduced, programmers feel uneasy and often complaint that all fun is taken out of programming and that they become mere coders. The uneasiness goes away when the programmers see that structured systems give them more work to do, by bringing forward their responsibilities, during the designing stage.
- introducing structured techniques for analysis, design and development, starting at any point in a project.

4.8   The Rapid Building Method

A quick method for building systems, using structured design techniques make for better systems, at lower costs, by providing techniques for detecting and correcting errors as early and as cheaply as possible.

Although quicker, it still means going through the structured analysis, designing, top-down development, structured coding and having structured Walkthroughs. What it means, is that the system engineer tries to cut down the unproductive use of professional time by matching what is possible with what is worth doing.

To manage such steps requires a lot of experience in the whole system development lifecycle and at each step the following thoughts ought to be raised:

- The system being built is of a technically excellent status, but is this what the users want?
- The users were given what they asked, but could the Analyst have done so much more for them?

In approaching the quick way of developing a system the analyst needs good probing techniques. He or she must find out the factors which stand in the way of achieving the objectives. The factors which would be impacted by better, faster, richer information.

It is a fact, that unlike other engineering projects, system engineering cannot produce a model. In complex construction projects, a scale model is built and everybody concerned can get a vivid idea of what the final building will look and how their interests will be served.

In information technology this can be done by diagrammatic representation, demonstration of dataflow diagrams and screen prototypes.

'Boxes' as symbols are used as the tools of structured analysis in a DFD (Dataflow Diagram) form, where they fit together as a logical model of a system, at any level of detail.

The symbols involved are:

- External Entity (outside the boundary),
- Dataflow,
- Process (Each process within the boundary can be exploded),
- Datastore.

The quick building method relies heavily on the composition of Structured English, which in turn depends on the:

- functional decomposition,
- lowest level - decomposed DFD,
- entity diagram,
- descriptions.

The details extracted from all four above will 'sieve' into Structured English. These in turn, have their own conditions and actions:

        IF condition - 1
                THEN action - A
        ELSE (not condition - 1)
                action - B.

In nested 'Ifs', using 'AND-IF', the following example may help:

        IF you need a holiday
                AND-IF you can afford it
                        AND-IF you have somewhere to go
                                THEN take a holiday
                        ELSE (you have nowhere to go)

As a rule of thumb, in writing Structured English please do not nest more than three levels.

The role of the Analyst in all this is of great importance. A well trained, ethical individual with about five years experience will be able to:

- help in devising the system versions and speak for the users' interests,
- explain the top-down development concept to the user community,
- ensure management support for timely systems development,
- exert pressure for frequent, full integration of sub-systems,
- ensure that the sub-system is developed top-down,
- act as the users' representative in accepting each version.

Based on the procedures standards defined in the next chapter, the Analyst will carry out an analysis of the present systems operations and identify the problems. This exercise will include the:

Andreas Sofroniou

- computer system,
- manual system
- combination of both.

This stage will be followed by the specification of the required system where the requirements are consolidated and the chosen option is defined in detail. In parallel to this, the required data structure is created.

4.9 Structured English

Sometimes known as 'pseudocode' and 'tight (or strict) English' this pre-programming tool bridges the gap between the logical and physical stages. Together with the processes, functional decomposition and the data structures, it serves as the 'sieve' into programming, especially if a 4th generation language (4GL) is to be used for constructing the system.

By following the structured English route, the programmers are given the opportunity to review the work, prior to accepting the design of the system. With the programmers' contribution and critique, the system stands a better chance by making any necessary alterations, before the actual implementation. Thus, less post-implementational maintenance and costly repairs.

In constructing the modules, programs can be made up out of suitable combinations of step-by-step instructions; like MOVE or ADD, binary decisions; IF, THEN, ELSE and loops. The logical processes defined in structured analysis are just that, programs for execution.

These few structures provide the basis for Structured Programming, which gets part of its effectiveness from the simplification and standardisation that comes from using structures, rather than the great variety permitted by a programming language. There are even more benefits, if the specifications can be written using the same approach, structured English.

As a rule, there are three main 'structures' in structured programming:

1. Sequential instructions: This structure covers any instructions which have no repetition, or branching, i.e.

   'multiply hours-worked by pay-rate to get gross-pay,
   dispatch products to customer's ship-to-address,
   add postage and package charges to total on invoice.'

   It is sometimes necessary to include descriptions of terms used, as in the above 'postage and package charges'.

2. Decision instructions: The standard format for a decision is the structure: IF, THEN, ELSE.

   Each action can be a set of sequential instructions, or loop, or another decision. To expand an earlier example:

   ```
   IF      you need a break
      THEN IF     you can afford the break
              THEN    go on a holiday
           ELSE (you cannot afford going away)
                      decorate the flat
      ELSE    you do not need the break carry on working.
   ```

3. Repetition (loop) instructions: This structure applies to any situation in which an instruction is repeated until some desired result is obtained.

   For instance, on an invoice with a number of items each listed on a separate line with quantity and unit price, it could be specified with 'REPEAT', as :

   ```
   REPEAT          extend-item-line until all lines have been extended.
   ```

Andreas Sofroniou

The extend-item-line to be described as: Multiply quantity by unit price to get line total.

While the analyst should specify the repetitions as part of the logical function, it is wise to involve the programmer in setting up loops. As the analyst is concerned with the logical processing of each data structure, the programmer is concerned with the physical processing of a stream of structures. In this way, the definition of loops becomes more important.

When the logic is written in English sentences, using the capitalisation and indentation conventions, it is known as Structured English.

In summary, the conventions are:

- the logic of processes expressed as combination of sequential, decision, case and repetition structures,
- keywords IF, THEN, ELSE, REPEAT, UNTIL, should be capitalised and indented to show their hierarchy,
- blocks of instructions to be grouped and given a meaningful name describing their function.

At the beginning of this section, 'pseudocode' and 'tight English' were mentioned. It is only fair to add that these are not the same as 'structured English'. A process defined in structured English is not a computer program. The conventions of structured English, but without the detailed syntax of English and the 'almost-code' notation is known as 'pseudocode'.

To specify a program in pseudocode, a programmer needs to be able to handle initialisation and termination, read and write to files, handle end-of-file and specify counters and flags.

In pseudocode, the programmer distinguishes the DO-WHILE loop structure from the REPEAT-UNTIL loop structure. The DO-WHILE loop implies that the termination test is made before the body of the loop is executed. The REPEAT-UNTIL implies that the body of the loop is executed before the test is made.

It is important to note that the pseudocode represents a very detailed program design. Especially in an environment where all data structure and data elements are defined in a data dictionary, the task of translating pseudocode into COBOL, or similar languages, is relatively a simple one.

Where as pseudocoding can be beneficial where COBOL and other similar programming languages are present, the convention of 'tight English' can be poor for its use in programming environment.

The unfamiliar notation of tight English is not ideal for presentation to users. The main difficulty with tight English, is that it is hard to write until the logic of a process is worked out in structured English and understood in detail in terms of the structures; sequence, decision, case, repetition.

This section dealt with structured English and the Analysts together with Programmer as the professionals who are supposed to deal with this activity. The training of both should include structured English, as this will bring both closer in their work for the development of the system, in its full lifecycle; the logical and physical stages

5: Managing Systems Development

5.1   Systems Management

The majority of organisations recognise that the effective use of information is vital to their success. Successful companies build enormous knowledge bases that reside in their corporate files, their information centres and in the brains of their busy executives. This knowledge and experience is the organisation's power base and their competitive edge.

To remain competitive they must be able to find information at the right time, in the right place and in the format that is easy to use..

The management of the information systems must ensure:

- the availability of the information,
- the services that enable this,
- effective use of technology,
- the supply of the skills and time needed,

When the IT department manages the information derived from the systems, effectively, the company in turn gains real value from information. The IT department and its management of information must maintain a leading position in the specialised world of commercial computing.

The IT department will certainly benefit by having a network of specialists providing knowledge, experience and technical skills to suit most types of company demands.

In managing IT professionally, the benefits will include the:

- capturing of the knowledge already in the organisation,
- making this knowledge accessible to those running the company,
- developing the appropriate strategic plans and systems,
- protection of the information supplied by the systems,
- accuracy and recoverability of all data,
- recruitment, training and developing the system engineers.

Instant access to corporate information means better decisions, reduced costs and increased profits. To facilitate such a service, the IT department must work with a wide range of other departments and their staff. Many of the users are looking for help, or advice from the information management area.

This means that the IT staff must be prepared to undertake all sizes of projects, their development and the management of such systems. This entails a project management system which, together with the chosen methodology, will ensure the success of the information services.

5.2   Structured Management Methods

Many users believe that a project must involve computers in some way. However, a much broader view is required when one considers that a project is set up to deliver a business product. In other words, a projects temporary, which only exists to deliver something considered worthwhile to the business.

The resulting product may be for any application (manual or otherwise, clerical, management style, production of goods, engineering in general) , including a computer system. In this case, the environment created and the work done to deliver the product, is a project.

In some cases, projects may not deliver what was expected and costly investment produces few benefits. It is little wonder that things go wrong and projects fail, not because people are ineffective, but because of the sheer complexity of project management.

Andreas Sofroniou

Some of the problems which may be familiar to management at all levels, are:

- no standard approach to project management,
- lack of communication,
- inadequate planning,
- unclear project objectives,
- uncontrolled change,
- shortage of experienced project managers,
- inadequate team building,
- inefficient staff motivation,
- poor quality standards.

Over the years it has become recognised that there is a common thread running through the management of projects. Much of this is common sense and it is the formulation of this rational thinking and management good practice, into a structure, which gives rise to project methods.

There are many project management methods available, each of which is characterised by the way in which it provides principles, procedures and techniques for the management of projects. Methods utilise existing standard techniques as well as introducing their own unique features.

The number of project failures can be dramatically reduced by the proper application of a structured project management method. A method which provides project management principles and processes to address the problems.

Structured management methods have evolved in private and government sectors since the late seventies. Such a management method is PRINCE (PRoject IN Controlled Environment). It is owned by the CCTA (Central Computer and Telecommunications Agency) and it is offered as a publicly available open product. This means that it is available to anyone and can be used without permission to apply it and without license, or fee of any kind.

A number of project management methods provide a variety of approaches. Traditional project management and other management methods plan and control against a list of activities. Some specially designed for the information systems project environment. Such procedures are applied to many types and sizes of project. This, therefore, gives the advantage of common standards being applied to the management of systems projects.

Using a management method will ensure that a system is built for the users and for the benefit of the business. Quality is of paramount importance to all IT departments. There are a few official national and international standards in information management, so an important feature of the structured management method approach is to create a de facto environment where standards can interrelate as they evolve.

The features of a structured management method can be summarised by a few basic facts:

- it brings together many standard procedures and techniques,
- provides a standard for management which can be applied to all types and sizes of a project,
- can be adapted to suit deferring projects, existing procedures and cultural attitudes,
- a quality approach to project management.

A structured management method provides management with the ability to react swiftly and efficiently to business and strategy changes, to understand what projects and studies are in hand and their interrelationships both, with each other and with the overall strategy. It, also, provides an effective way of controlling costs and resources at the business level.

All management methods demand the participation of senior management in any type of project. From the initial stage to the phase where a completed system is handed over to the user community. A project, also, needs the involvement of quality assurance and other support staff, where all the participants form the steering committee and the support groups.

The committee and all participating follow a project management method, comprising integrated procedures, based on a number of principles and documented in a set of procedural manuals.

The principles are:
- organisation,
- planning,
- controls,
- stages,
- product based approach,
- quality.

The overall objective of the structured management method is to enable the right people to make the right decision at the right time. This formally enforces the involvement and commitment of the business, users and technical interest in a project.

It creates a flexible organisational hierarchy of:
- people representing business and users,
- project manager, responsible to the committee for day to day management,
- project team members,
- people providing support and assuring delivery of quality products.

Plans are the basis of the management of any project. They provide the benchmark of information required for decision making, controlling, communicating and reporting.

Plans at each level address:
- scope,
- products,
- quality,
- risk management,
- timescale,
- resources,
- costs,
- controls.

Project control is carried out at two levels, by:
- formal assessment meetings,
- the project manager at checkpoint meetings.

The objectives of each meeting are defined and guidance is provided on the agenda and procedures. In certain projects, it is recognised that there may be a requirement to control the work of the project in more detail.

Project management methods are concentrating on the things to be produced, rather than the activities required to produce them. These things are called products and the approach ensures that all products are identified and clearly defined before proceeding with activity planning. It is a significant aid to better estimating and planning.

A structured management method, also, provides detailed guidance on the procedures and techniques required to apply the principles.

These procedures and techniques include:
- project initiation,
- product planning techniques,
- business case,
- quality review,
- configuration management,
- change control,
- documentation.

The application of the procedures and techniques is flexible and it is this aspect which makes a management method practical and successful.

5.3   Management Of Projects

A project management system should be utilised on all sizeable projects undertaken. A Project Manager should be appointed, responsible for the agreement and delivery of project products to agreed deadlines throughout the project's lifecycle.

The main project management issues include:

- proper user, staff and management training,
- management commitment,
- budgets,
- user and expert time,
- identify key users,
- schedule time for analysis and design,
- establish metrics,
- small teams.
- testing implementation and handover to users.

The Project Manager should produce a weekly Status Report which will be provided one day prior to a weekly Progress Meeting.

This report will have the following format:

- milestones, summary report of the current and previous status of milestones,
- progress, a narrative of progress,
- Changes to the project baseline, including change notices,
- issues, details reported for current week and the status of those previously reported,
- variances in either time, or effort for any milestone,
- resource usage for the week,
- external factors that may impact upon progress, but not within the control of the project management,
- cost reports of any costs incurred during the week, excluding resource costs and known regular costs,
- objectives and risks for the next period,
- recommendations and issues for discussion.

The weekly meeting should take place between:

- the user Project Manager, or representative,
- the system Project Manager, or representative.

During the project lifecycle, project issues can occur which require analysis, documentation and resolutions. Project issues fall into those that occur during the:

- development and delivery of the system,
- operational life of the system.

Any change to the requirements, or to any document once it has been formally agreed, is subject to the following change control procedures:

- a change control notice will be raised by the user requesting the change,
- an estimate of the impact of the change on the schedule and costing of the project will be prepared by the system Project Manager,
- the change details will be transmitted to the users representative for authorisation,

- if the change is authorised, then the change control notice will be annotated by the member of the project team, who implements the change to indicate that it has been completed. A copy will then be filed with the documentation affected,
- the documentation itself will be updated to reflect the change, with update pages sent to all nominated parties,
- all changes during the project, whether by the user, or system developer will be controlled by the IT project area.

Throughout the life of the project, reviews of critical documents are necessary. The procedures for review of these documents are as follows:

- all critical documents will be reviewed within the project team structure to ensure adherence to the project standards,
- the quality to be randomly selected and reviewed by the Assurance Manager,

In case of controlled documents, this will include a check that the documents have the following details:

- document identification,
- document name,
- name of system Project Manager,
- distribution list,
- current version.

The strategy of the system acceptance will be defined by the user. The subsequent plan and test scripts will be based upon the standards. As part of a quality management system, a senior manager undertakes the auditing of the project. The quality auditor operates outside the design and build team structures.

Before delivery of the system, a training schedule for the users will be agreed. Additionally, prior to any handing over, the system will be tested and should any problems arise, these will be reported and remedied before the users sign off.

5.4   Recruitment And Interviewing In Computing

With the state-of-the-art in commercial computing, the accelerated progress in technology and the demand made on more systems development, the IT management find themselves increasingly occupied in the selection of larger number of specialised staff. Such is the great weight on IT managers, to fulfill new job responsibilities and to replace those who leave for greener pastures.

The vacancies for system engineers are constantly increasing, at such a rate that a new industry has developed. Additional to the traditional recruitment, the demand for the supply of contractors, mainly for systems analysis and programming, has increased in proportions. Agencies for freelancers are now deeply rooted as a service to IT.

The contracting analysts/programmers are in their thousands and agencies in their hundreds. The cost to the organisation for such a service is huge, often enough remuneration paid being higher than what the business directors are paid. Frequently more than the IT manager gets. With such numbers of candidates involved and an unknown expertise at that, the systems managers are faced with the additional responsibility of frequent interviews and uncertainty as to what kind of know-how they will obtain from contractors.

The agencies do not have the knowledge to scrutinise every system engineer on their registers. It is a well known fact that the agents submit the CVs of individuals without even checking on the contractor's experience. The agencies arrange for the interviews between the company's managers and the freelancers over the telephone. For this kind of service the agencies receive between 20% and 40% of the contracting fees. The larger, established contracting agencies have a firm charge of 33% commission.

The IT management and their staff are faced with the overload of interviews. It is an under-estimated task. With all the pressures from within the systems areas, it is a wonder how systems can be developed and become operational within the quoted timescales and costs.

THE MANAGEMENT OF COMMERCIAL COMPUTING

As an example, using the two extremes of the systems engineering professions of Analysts and Programmers. It is of paramount importance to use the right techniques for interviewing systems staff. In hiring systems engineers, it must be remembered that an analyst is the person who keeps in touch with the users and the programmer is the one that builds the system.

The analyst must be an out-going person, a good mixer. A person who can get on with other people, easily collect information and details and must be a good systems representative. The psychological personality type of an extrovert thinker.

On the other extreme, bear in mind that the programmer has to decipher the documents the analyst produces, in order to start constructing the required system. This makes the programmer the psychological personality of an introvert sensation type.

There are many other types of professionals within systems engineering. Designers, database administrators, operators, strategists, and a few more. In interviewing, therefore, the interviewer will be helped enormously if he/she makes a few notes beforehand regarding the type of person needed to fill in the responsibilities within the systems professions.

In interviewing, handing out a short narrative and asking the interviewee to turn it into diagrams and programming coding is not on. The candidate must be relaxed, made to feel wanted, important and then prompted to expand on items relevant to the vacancy.

Systems engineering is such a modern profession, its responsibilities and qualities are hardly known to psychologists psychometrists and professional recruiters. For instance, one cannot rely on aptitude testing alone, as there are no set rules. Experience in systems areas and knowing what is needed is the best guide and basis for the interview.

Within the various scales of recruitment are the newcomers to the professions of systems management. The graduates of IT 'hybrid' management and the MBAs, whose degree material is based on traditional management. Commercial computing demands organisational experience gained within business functions relating to systems.

The young graduates of the first degree education, can be recruited with the proviso that they get trained within the business parameters. It is true that the new universities in their computing sciences subjects cover methodologies, databases and programming, but the question still prevails. The extend of commercial experience embedded in the lecturers and their tutorials and those running the academic departments. Let it be stressed that this statement refers to the business computing and systems development in the commercial world.

Universities have progressed enormously in their research on artificial intelligence and other fields such as parallelism. The outside world still runs systems on mainframes and applications as required by the users. The modern construction of business systems and tools developed, suit the personalities and the abilities of those who use these applications.

Faced with such problems, the IT management pays a lot of attention to interviewing. After all, like any other recruitment, employing a human being (permanent or contractor) is still a big investment of time, costs and other resources.

It must be added, that the interviewing techniques in commercial computing are applied to applicants for vacant positions, as well as the users who ask for new systems, the repairing of an existing one, or the extraction of the data based information.

Interviewing is the most commonly used way of acquiring basic concepts and requirements from the users. It is an activity that needs careful planning and execution. It is crucial to plan an interview to ensure that it is as productive as possible.

Whether interviewing an applicant for a vacancy, or a user for his/her requirements, it is worthwhile bearing the following in mind:

- ensure that the interviewee is prepared for the interview,
- notify the subject to be covered,

- the time and location of the interview,
- probable length of the interview,
- ensure that a room is ready, away from the interviewee's workplace, thus minimising distractions,
- make the interviewee comfortable with the computing terminology and jargon,
- build a rapport, listen and show interest.

As an interviewer, practise the art of relaxation on you and then apply the technique to the candidate. Remember that the users interviewees may offer details on what they think you want to know. A good analyst will steer the discussion to the domain of interest. Whereas a job applicant will be nervous, anxious and feel as if on the receiving end.

5.5   Project Control In Developing Systems

Businesses have problems which they need to solve. They, also, have requirements which altogether enables the smooth running of their environment. To establish the appropriate running of the business organisation, projects need to be set.

An organisation is probably undergoing significant change. Changes span functional boundaries, case conflict and concern and present a major risk to the business and those managers responsible for the development of systems. Many companies are now adopting a project-based approach to managing the change of systems and their development.

Managers of today and of the future, require skills in managing projects. These skills are supplementary to the line management skills. A company needs to enhance business planning and control structures to explicitly link system implementation to business led projects and programmes.

A project in information technology is a temporary situation within the working groups (the system users) and the computing management, with the objective of delivering a product. The resulting product relies on the project progress and how it is approached in its scope to deliver.

For a project to be successful it needs:

- management at all levels,
- team building and staff motivation,
- planning and controls,
- quality standards to follow,
- communication between users and management,
- objectives and scope,
- adequate skills and experienced resources,
- explicit documentation and training.

Unlike existing systems operational management, where one deals with established computer services, project management encounters the unfamiliar, new problems and needs for change.

In managing a project, a list of activities will not be enough. The project must be product-based. A methodology needs to be followed, procedures to be applied. The appropriate procedures, therefore, give the advantage of common standards being applied to the management of all projects, with directional emphasis to meeting the corporate objectives.

Always remembering that a system is built with quality and that the application of the procedures and techniques must be flexible and practical:

- for the users,
- to fulfill a process,
- benefit the business function,

Project management supports the implementation of the business strategies with explicit link to the development plan. This provides management with the ability to react swiftly and efficiently to any changes, to understand the project stages and steps in hand and their relationship with each other. It, also, provides an effective way of controlling costs and resources at all levels.

The appropriate analysis and design methodology will assist the project team members to concentrate on the system components to be produced. It enables the management and the analysts to identify and clearly define all the development phases. It is, also, a significant contributor to quality, better estimating and planning.

This means that a systems manager and his/her team members need to establish project control standards, which will specifically include:

1. purpose,
2. scope,
3. input,
4. planning,
5. progress control.

1. Purpose:

The purpose of the project control standards is to define the standard to be used within system development for managing the project in terms of project planning and progress control. The objectives of project management being:

- establish clear objectives and scope for a project,
- ensure roles and responsibilities are well defined and understood,
- break work down into schedules and deliverables,
- plan how an individual project will achieve the implementation of the required end product within a progressively refined and agreed schedule and budget.

A project control framework is necessary within which project management skills and techniques are exercised.

2. Scope:

This standard addresses Project Control in a new system development environment, i.e. a multi-team situation with Team Leaders and an overall Project Manager.

It covers the planning of each phase for each team and its members and the progressing of those plans.

3. Input:

The inputs will vary with the size and stage of development:

- Terms of Reference (ToR, for a new project) and Project Initiation Document (PID),
- key documentation from earlier phases (for an existing project)
- procedures manual

4. Planning:

The following steps describe a team leader's project control, carried out at the start of a project, or when rescheduling (as a result of supplying more tasks, or changing estimates).

- Task Identification. A source of information for this will be the overall project plan and the activities listed.
- Estimating. Estimating for project control planning is carried out using the bottom-up approach, starting with the steps involved and building upwards. When all tasks have been identified and estimated, an overall schedule can be drawn, which accounts for resource constraints, deadlines and overheads.

- Scheduling. The basics of scheduling are to take the information from task identification, sizing and resource allocation and to build a schedule which meets the necessary timescales.

5. Progress Control:

The Project Control system and progress meetings are the principal mechanisms for monitoring and controlling the progress of a project.

- Progress Meetings. Aside from the informal contact maintained between a team leader and team members, each person should receive a regular progress meeting, on an one-to-one basis. Also, each team leader should meet with the project manager on a similar basis.
- Team Meetings. A regular weekly meeting of all team members is important, in order to maintain communication and to resolve issues where input is required.
- Outstanding Issues. As projects progress, design issues may emerge which require a solution. At the end of the development, any loose ends not resolved can be passed to the support team for future enhancements to the system.
- Rescheduling. Even the best planned project may have its scope changed by changes in requirements, or late design changes. Changes of this type can cause disruption which outweigh the benefits they provide, so it is important to keep them to a minimum.

5.6   Systems Development Procedures

The system specification procedures form the basis within the conventional business environment for setting out the standards for system development. They describe a step by step approach to developing and implementing computer systems. They define the documents to be produced, the controls to be applied and the tasks to be performed.

The intention is that these procedures be applied flexibly. On the other hand, the phases are designed for sequential development, with the output from one phase being the input to the next, all leading to the eventual implementation of the system. Project plans should be drawn up to suit the particular project and then adhered to.

The procedures define the paths that will be followed in projects set up to develop computer systems. A project is, thus, described in terms of its major divisions (Phases), its Control Points, the Activities that are accomplished in each phase and the Tasks that go to make up those activities.

A project starts with an initiation and ends with a review and user training. The Project Initiation Document (PID) will incite the feasibility study and the terms of reference. The review will include the report to the users and the appropriate steps for the system training and the training manual distributed to all the users involved in the running of the system-to-be.

Otherwise, the project has the following phases:

1. Business Analysis: Users' business Problems and Requirements and the initial top level Dataflow Diagram.
2. Systems Analysis: System Proposal, Functional Decomposition, Dataflow Diagram, Logical Data Structure and Process Descriptions,
3. Design Options: Technical Design Options,
4. Functional Analysis: Process Model, Detailed Dataflow Diagram and Process Descriptions,
5. Data Analysis: Data Model, Entity Life History,
6. Physical Design/Build, System Specification, Program Code.

The system development lifecycle, in outlining the activities to be followed and the tasks to be carried out in a project, provides the framework for planning and defining a project.

The development lifecycle does not ensure that projects will meet a particular level of quality, nor does it ensure that work carried out will be both, efficient and effective. That is a matter of how people perform and it is the goal of project management to make sure that conditions exist for them to be efficient and effective.

The framework of the lifecycle with its different phases, offers some guidance on when project management should be applied. Each phase has a beginning, middle and end. Project management procedures are ongoing and required to fit in with the dimensions of the workday and reporting cycles.

Project management is a series of activities that are carried out during a project by the leader:

- planning,
- estimating,
- monitoring,
- reporting,
- quality control,
- resource allocation,
- communication.

The performance of any computer department can only be judged by the service given to the system users. This clearly means business change through projects. It involves people and the experience they carry with them. Experience in system building when a company needs it most; when this type of people, the best in the organisation are in short supply and great demand. They are usually, therefore, not available when needed for a critical new project - to develop the long awaited system.

5.7   Systems Specification

The System Specification starts as far back as Systems Analysis and is not completed until programming begins. A standard is required for conducting systems design because a uniform approach is needed across all projects to ensure understanding and consistency.

The standard outputs are required as input to programming activities. The systems specifications, therefore, need to be written in a rigorous and consistent manner to ensure that all user requirements are catered for and all business processing is completely and accurately defined and documented.

The following may be input to system specification:
- current, systems documentation and specifications,
- user requirements documentation and proposals,
- system proposal from system analysis phase,
- process descriptions, dataflow diagrams and layouts from the functional analysis phase,
- minutes of meetings with users.

The System Specification is the phase where the lowest level dataflow diagrams and descriptions from process analysis are pulled together.

5.8   Process Analysis

The aim is to reach a detailed logical design sufficient for all specification work. A standard is required for conducting process analysis because a uniform approach is needed across all projects. It concentrates on processes rather than data. Thorough process analysis encourages understanding of the system and user environment. The outputs from the process analysis are required for the system design processes.

There can be many inputs into process analysis depending on the nature and complexity of the project. The following may be input to process analysis:
- systems documentation and specifications from the current system,
- user requirements and proposals
- decomposition of dataflow diagrams.

The dataflow diagram is a powerful input to design because it identifies the data flows, data stores and processing involved. The technique is top-down; an overview followed by increasingly lower levels of detail.

5.9   System Reviews

The purpose of a review is to define the process for understanding what is needed and as means of checking the quality of work throughout the systems development lifecycle.

The objectives of holding a review of a piece of work are to:
- ensure the work meets its requirements,
- trap errors as early as possible,
- provide a focus on outstanding issues which lie in the pathway to completion of a given task,
- check adherence to standards.

It is clear that in practice it would not be appropriate to subject all outputs to the same level of review and several variants of the review process are required.

The different levels of review allow for the:
- importance of the review material,
- authority of the attendees,
- level at which the review is documented,
- formality with which the review is held.

5.10 Physical Design

Physical design converts the results of process and data design into an implementable computer solution and defines the computer/clerical interface. This is evaluated against the requirements and amended as appropriate.

The scope of the physical design is to cover the technical design of application systems. It concentrates on the design of the system processes, rather than the design of databases.

The following may be input to systems design:

- current systems documentation and specifications,
- user requirements and solutions,
- system proposal from analysis phase,
- process descriptions, dataflow diagrams and layouts from functional analysis phase.

Requirements often change during the design phase and new ones emerge. In addition, it often raises more questions requiring further analysis. Therefore, the final design may only be arrived at through several iterations of logical and physical design.

5.11 Quick Dataflow Diagramming

Dataflow diagrams (DFDs) are used for process analysis, to show the logical:

- system processes, hierarchy and their relationships,
- datastores, the system's data 'at rest',
- data flows, the system's data 'in motion' between two processes, or between a process and a datastore.

To present a complete system description, additional documentation is necessary for each flow, each datastore, and each process.

It is the DFD which structures the analysis process and drawing the DFD helps the Analyst to:

- deal with the information collected during data gathering, in an orderly manner,
- avoid being overwhelmed by detail and losing sight of the overall picture,
- document the proposed system in a convenient format as input to design,
- communicate with users.

In diagramming, the following conventions apply to drawing dataflow diagrams:

- External Entity, usually represented by a circle outside the boundary. This is the source, or destination of data outside the area under study. If the circle has a line across the corner, then the external entity is used elsewhere and has been duplicated for diagramming convenience.
- Data Flow, depicted by an arrow and a description put alongside the arrow. The arrow shows direction of flow. Flows are labelled with a meaningful name describing content of the flow, not the document or report carrying the data.
- Process, usually represented by a rectangle, it can be a manual process or computerised. Processes are labelled with an appropriate and clear-cut name, which should be a verb followed by an object phrase. A process 'box' should be labelled for easy reference. This should reflect the top-down hierarchy. (Process: 1, 1.1, 1.1.1/1.1.2/1.1.3, Process: 2, etc.)
- Datastore, symbolised by an open-ended rectangle. A name for the datastore that is meaningful to users is written inside the symbol. Datastores should be numbered sequentially and prefixed by the letter 'D'.

In drawing a DFD the following must always be considered:

- The highest level picture of the system is called a 'context diagram' and consists of one box representing the system under study.
- External Entities are shown outside the boundary line, along with the flows between the study system and the externals.
- Having agreed a context diagram with the user management, a first level DFD is created containing high level functions.
- The functions on the first level DFD are then exploded by creating another DFD for each particular process. Each further level clarifies the activities within a system and shows an increasing level of detail in the activities themselves and the dataflows that connect them.
- In a new system partitioning should go to the level where each process box corresponds to a specific process. Partitioning is an iterative process. It takes several reviews to get to a perfect diagram.
- With partitioning it is always difficult to know when a sufficient level of detail has been reached.

  The following guidelines may help:

  - More than five flows into a process may indicate that the activity is over complex, although up to seven may be accommodated. Less than three, may indicate insufficient information.

  - The narrative description should not take more than a couple of pages.

  - The process should relate to units of work recognised by the user.

  - Generally, it should be possible to identify a single input that drives the process.

  - Often, there is only one major output.

- DFDs should be kept as simple as possible to avoid confusion. A good rule of thumb is no more than seven processes per page. If there are more than this, it probably means that there are more details than necessary. To be on the safe side, create another level by exploding one process into a lower level DFD.
- Symbols should be duplicated on the diagram to avoid crossing lines. A duplicate should be marked with a line on the left hand side of the symbol.
- Avoid partitioning according to company organisation, as the diagrams show functions not organisations.

5.12   Program Design

Before they are coded, programs need to be designed. There needs to be a structure which shows how and where the processes diagrammed in the DFD and described in the System Specification are to be performed.

Structured English is used to represent the design. This is a simplified form of English, presented in defined manner. Within the structure so formed, normal English is used, although in as succinct a form as possible.

The relevant systems specification proceeds to a program design ready for coding. To enable this, the following inputs are necessary:

- decomposition diagram,
- DFDs at the program or transaction level,
- system specification,
- system flowchart,
- data structure diagram.

A program design which is structured is easier to maintain and understand. The structuring of the design means principally that the design should be driven by the flows of input and output data.

The program designer or programmer should arrange for regular program and code Walkthroughs with another programmer/designer. The walkthrough session should check:

- adherence to programming standards,
- that the code matches the design structure,
- that the code performs the processing defined in the system specification,
- that database accessing is correct.

Program designing and programming in general, requires disciplined management since this needs clearly defined objectives to fulfill the overall project.

Project management must, therefore, ensure that the investment of resources, time and effort are fully justified and fulfilled. This includes program definition and the setting up of efficient structures. Whatever the requirements, experience is of major importance in helping and controlling programming

6: Commercial Systems Packages

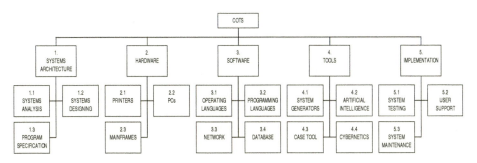

6.1 Packages

Some organisations have always followed the principle of 'build rather than attempt to buy'. Recent studies established that this trend has now started to change. Such studies have shown that the U.S.A. Department of Defense (DoD), the North Atlantic Treaty Organisation (NATO), the U.K. Ministry of Defence (MOD), the Central Computer and Telecommunications Agency (CCTA) and other government departments are seriously optimising the use of (Commercial Off-The-Shelf) COTS packages.

The USA DoD firmly explored the role of COTS software in the domain of large, real time, mission-critical systems. Regarding the networking of their hardware and software environments the DoD encouraged their suppliers to convene and resolve the communicational difficulties.

The NATO are establishing guidelines in the deployment of COTS software. COTS software provides a significant opportunity to NATO to control and lower software development costs, but with reservations regarding continuity of support, inconsistency among packages and integration with NATO specific software.

The UK MOD has not undertaken a firm commitment to the overall issue of COTS. Specific studies in large systems in the three forces have shown that there is a preferred route towards commercial packages. In the case of the Naval Logistics System of the Upkeep project, having prepared the users requirements, it is hoped that the majority of the modules will be served by commercial packages.

The Central Computer and Telecommunications Agency (CCTA) has already established certain standards, regarding CASE Tools (System Engineer), Structured Methodology (SSADM - Structured System and Design Methodology) and the Project Control method of PRINCE. The guidelines are used by most Government Departments and CCTA expertise is made available in the form of consultative service.

6.2 Commercial Off-the-shelf (COTS)

COTS packages are developed by commercial companies for a variety of applications and a wide range of users. The user market is increasing, therefore COTS will be cheaper to acquire. A procured package can be flexible and reliable, if based on well defined requirements. The chosen software are maintained by the vendor and can represent the state-of-the-art.

The usage of COTS packages have gained some acceptance in the U.K., as a cost effective approach. The supply and maintenance costs are lower than the bespoke developed systems. Originally COTS software was confined to operating languages and database management systems. Application-based packages, such as office automation and networking are now becoming standard, both in the large organisations and government departments.

By using COTS software, the development costs are lowered. But supplier support, inconsistency among packages and integration with other existing systems are difficult. Criteria for proper selection and management are required.

Andreas Sofroniou

Some COTS packages are built for specific applications. This restricts portability and any attempt to change any of the facilities will jeopardise the set standards and affect the lower costs.

Therefore, there is a need to set a suite of rules regarding the selection of COTS. These would lead to the development of guidelines to the Project Managers and users at large. COTS products to be selected with the same level of effort as that input into the formal system analysis and designing exercises. Failure to do so, will cost as much, if not more, than the traditional system development.

It is of vital importance to remember that, the larger the system required, the more difficult it will be to choose the right COTS package and less the chances of fulfilling the system requirements. The smaller the amount of logical requirements, the easier it will be to select the appropriate ready-to-use product.

Wherever the requirements are of large proportions, especially where a mainframe-based system is needed, it is advisable to build rather than attempt to buy a packaged system.

6.3   The Integration Of Packages

Great importance is placed on the integration of packages and the re-usability of software. The basic system components will have to be carefully chosen and comply with the Open System Environment (OSE) base standards. As companies adopt new standards, the framework would need to be revised accordingly.

It is the large organisations' experience that COTS products do not always fulfill the requirements. Even if such products meet the set standards they do not always operate in conjuction with each other.

Many data entities (data types) need changing in order to communicate with each other. In addition, different data groups will require different storage, transmission and display strategies.

The COTS market is constantly changing. This creates new products, much faster than the commercial world would be able to acquire systems. Hardware and software become obsolete by the time a system becomes operational.

Although vendors claim standards compliance, in practice many problems have occurred. Conformance evaluation to test and validate standards, is recommended.

When COTS products have been selected, their evolution should be closely monitored. If these products are no longer meeting the state-of-the-art, the framework should allow easy replacement by other COTS products.

To approve any purchases of COTS packages, a company ought to take into consideration the following:

- The environment under which the package is to run,
- The quality and the maturity of the software,
- The standing of its supplier,
- The prospects for its long-term support,
- The adherence to OSE standards,
- Portability to other architectures.

In a bespoke system, security can be integrated as required. With COTS products, this is rather difficult and the system/s can become vulnerable.

The application of COTS software in smaller company systems can often be considered a more cost-effective approach across the whole life-cycle, than the development of new purpose-built software.

There are a number of issues which require investigation in order to facilitate the choice of the most appropriate COTS products. These issues must be considered in detail, in order to develop procurement guidelines, procedures and selection criteria for the use of COTS software.

In many larger companies, there is a preference to procure software rather than to develop software from scratch. The initial procurement costs do not necessarily determine the final savings. In order to achieve economies over a longer period, COTS procurement need to be well managed.

Current practice in international organisations for MIS software, calls for the use of COTS as far as practicable. This is based on the increase in reliability anticipated from software which have been succesfully used elsewhere and, secondly, a decrease in procurement cost compared with the development of a specifically tailored system.

6.4   Experience In COTS

In a recent presentation on COTS, the DoD Naval Undersea Warfare Center, U.S.A., explored the role of COTS software in the domain of large, real time, mission-critical systems.

In the case of networking hardware and software, the DoD encouraged the suppliers to achieve compatibility among themselves. Based on this, it is hoped that the DoD will establish a commonality in the various packages.

A presentation by the USA DoD NUWC, refers to COTS as the umbrella for:

* electronics,
* development Tools,
* graphics,
* network,
* equipment.

The DoD describes COTS as being items that can be purchased through commercial, retail, or wholesale distribution for use as is. The procurement of such items can be extended to cover government off-the-shelf and modified COTS products.

The main question as to whether COTS software is the answer, remains as an issue for the DoD. There is no doubt that there are disadvantages in using COTS. The major ones being:

* No control over future product availability,
* Rights-in-data issues must be confronted,
* COTS products not tailored to specific applications.

For COTS to be successful, they must be useful packages at reasonable costs and compatible with the rest of the system environment.

Specific performance requirements cannot be met. Where performance is critical, modelling and simulation is needed to confirm that a COTS product is capable of meeting the requirements.

The size of COTS software for real-time is small. The shelf size for re-usable real-time operational software is even smaller. COTS software may be unavailable for demanding military applications.

There is a confusion between COTS re-use and Open Systems. Users think that because they have bought something commercial, they have achieved re-usability or an open system. Open systems facilitate the use of COTS, but the presence of COTS does not constitute an open system.

It is, also, stipulated that COTS is not a synonym for 'reusable'. COTS does not imply re-usability. The DoD 'Reuse Vision' is to guide the software community to a process-driven, domain-specific and architecture centred environment.

The fundamental underlying principles are on the reuse in specific domains, reuse oriented architectures and utilisation of an interconnected network of reuse libraries.

The DoD's experience in COTS software reuse includes the COTS relational database, minor COTS mathematics functions and COTS development tools to produce a large real-time system.

Some COTS lessons learned include COTS licensing agreements and to avoid modifying such packages. The DoD underlines the allocation of additional time and resource for tool modification and for resolution of COTS interface/performance problems.

With recent events and trends, the DoD is satisfied that the growth in industrial consortia aimed at establishing standards will benefit the COTS software and reuse programme.

In order to avoid excessive costs of building new systems, the DoD is prepared to accept common operational requirements, but the safety and security of COTS should remain bespoke.

6.5   The Commercial Off-the-shelf Studies

In the commercial world, COTS products are available for a widespread use in the market place. Many of the large systems have made use of COTS and most procurements have a COTS element.

COTS software is built by commercial companies for a large user market. Although COTS software is of general applicability, by nature; flexible, reliable and state-of-the-art, it restricts the user to specific computer configurations.

Adapted COTS software can no longer be called COTS, Many COTS packages allow for the incorporation of, or interfacing to user specific software in a third garneration language. Restrictions on calling routines between 4th generation languages (such as Ada) and COTS packages can exist.

As Ada is the 'defence' companies and government departments recommended 4GL for the development of new systems, it is important that an Ada interface is available. COTS packages can be categorised into four types and their interfacing with Ada is listed below:

- Ada COTS packages. These packages developed in Ada are easy to integrate with Ada application software,
- COTS packages with Ada interfaces. These packages are easy to integrate with Ada-based software,
- COTS software without an Ada interface. Many COTS packages provide interfaces to established languages like C, Fortran, Pascal, or COBOL, but not yet for Ada,
- COTS packages which do not require an Ada interface. Many COTS packages; word processors and spreadsheets run standalone and do not require an Ada interface.

British companies utilise COTS in the following application areas:

- accounting,
- CAD/CAM/CAE,
- configuration Management,
- costing/Cost Management,
- customer service,
- defence logistics,
- distribution,
- document management,
- executive information systems,
- human resources,
- library management,
- maintenance management,
- network management,
- logistics.

For some large systems there may be COTS packages which can fulfill some of the requirements. Experience shows that whatever the requirements, a substantial amount of work as a project is needed, prior to the acquisition of COTS.

As an example, a logistics project took two years, 50 people to establish the current method of work and the interpretation of the requirements into a logical documentation. Being a large required system, it will require a mixture of bespoke development with some modules replaced by COTS packages.

The reader will appreciate that the larger the system, the less the chances for an outright COTS solution. It must be stressed that the larger the system, the more difficult it is to select an appropriate COTS package.

Wherever the user requirements are of a substantial size the COTS solution will need to be looked into carefully, by collecting all relevant requirements, modelling these within a logical stage of development and then decide whether the required system can be:

- a complete bespoke system,
- partly bespoke and partly COTS,
- partly designed from scratch and partly modified COTS,
- divide the new system design into very small segments and then try COTS on a few individual small modules,
- modify the user requirements to suit the available COTS packages.

The latter may involve a totally new working method of what users are accustomed to. Therefore, the introduction of an extensive training course to cover the new modes of work, will be necessary.

The modification of requirements to suit COTS will reduce costs and substantially shorten the timescales. Large companies, from their experience, are preparing themselves for the adapt-your-requirements approach to COTS solutions.

In their current logistics exercises, known organisations have reached the point where the current systems and new requirements have been developed to stage 3 (the detailed study of what the users want), by using the SSADM (Structured
Systems And Design Methodology). The user accepted documentation has been presented for a possible COTS packages solution to a conglomeration of hardware, software and resourcing companies, who are currently looking for suitable COTS.

CASE (Computer-aided Software Engineering) Tools are already classified as COTS packages. A CASE tool, in turn, will assist in documenting and diagramming the COTS requirements. The MOD, almost all defence companies, many commercial organisations and financial institutions use the CCTA preferred System Engineer where the recommended methodology, SSADM, resides. The MOD is a dedicated user of SSADM, version 4, based on System Engineer. Certain sections of the DERA utilise the Object Oriented Methodology.

The challenge for the Information Technology, today, is to increase productivity, improve the quality of new applications and to maintain budget constraints. The solution can only be realised through a shared experience, with the companies developing COTS and the organisations who use the packages.

6.6   Reusability

Object technology, the Internet and information retrieval create new opportunities for software reuse. But there is always an up-front cost as reusable software costs more to build. Estimates show that reusable software requires three to ten times the development effort of one-off software. The payback for the vendor may not come for years. As a consequence, companies developing reusable products are not keen.

The search for reusable software is something that moved America's National Institute of Standards and Technology (NIST) Advance Technology Programme (ATP) to contribute $150 million into research on software reusability.

Approximately 200 software developers attended the third international conference on software reuse, held in November 1994, by the Institute of Electrical and Electronic Engineers.

Object-oriented programming can yield easily reused software components: class libraries and the pre-assembled kits of classes known as frameworks. The Internet enables software developers to distribute, advertise and search for software components worldwide. The problem is to find a business model of software distribution which works in the electronic environment.

Information retrieval presents the biggest technical challenge. What works for text will not necessarily work for software. English text consists of words with generally agreed meanings. Source code, however, is full of arbitrary names invented by programmers.

Interest in object-oriented programming (OOP) has soared. The biggest advantage of OOP is that objects can be re-used in different programs. Organisations and their policies on software reuse have generally adopted OOP languages, such as C++ or Smalltalk. But many companies strive for reuse without objects.

U.S. defence contracts often require the contractor to reuse software if suitable code exists and to make its own code available for reuse. Ada is the standard U.S. defence language and though it is strong on modularity and encapsulation, full OOP (object-oriented programming) will not be part of the language, until the adoption of Ada 9X, which currently, has Draft International Standard status.

Even COBOL may prove to be one of the more reasonable programming languages, for reasons unconnected with the planned OOP features of COBOL 97. Its verbose nature and English-like syntax tend to leave plenty of clues, not only to the mechanical function of a routine, but to its meaning and purpose. These clues might be picked up by information retrieval tools originally designed for use with natural-language text.

Object technology vendors such as Centerline Software and Hitachi Europe are among the first to deliver tools specifically designed to assist software reuse. This reflects customer demand who expect high rates of reuse when they adopt object technology. So the vendors have a powerful motive for making reuse work.

The re-use approach has obvious attractions in sharing development costs over a wider project base. Business process driven re-use may be a valid way of saving money. An agreement to evolve common procedures and approaches may prove beneficial for companies to join forces in utilising a common Information Systems strategy.

6.7   Open Standards

For the last twenty years institutions and government establishments in the western hemisphere have been pre-occupied with the standardisation of open systems. Systems in the 1980s were customised, in the 1990s governments accepted the commercial approach to systems development and in the year 2000, it is expected to proceed with open standards.

Open systems are receiving tremendous attention. Some of the claimed benefits from using open systems include:

- more competition leads to lower costs,
- the probability of schedule delay decreases,
- products are better tested, because they have more users,
- portable applications,
- interoperability in systems,
- faster technology insertion,
- foundation for system evolution.

The notion that open systems are a foundation for long-term system evolution is important. A goal to develop a disciplined framework for a system as that system evolves from new requirements, component upgrades and new technology. So open systems give a framework and the framework includes long-term supportability. Another related aspect to be listed is that the use open systems components represent a form of reuse.

An open system architecture is a collection of interacting software, hardware and human components, designed to satisfy stated needs. The American government policy is that 'agencies shall acquire commercial products and use commercial distribution systems whenever these systems satisfy the government's needs'. This serves to illustrate just how much the pendulum is swinging away from the government engaging in full-scale system development.

It is true that there are concerns about the use of open systems. Some of the claimed difficulties of open systems include:

- they cost too much,
- they are too risky (loss of control),
- they will never meet the exact user, performance and environment requirements,
- there are conformance and certification problems,
- there are supportability problems,
- they require continual investment,
- no prior experience in this field.

There are those who equate open systems with commercial products and believe that commercial products will not satisfy the requirements for performance. Hence, there are risks, including the risk of the quality of the implementation. This point has turned into a very interesting debate. One group believes that commercial products cannot meet performance and other requirements. the other group maintains that users at large have no unique requirements.

Open systems are driven by the modular use of components and modular creation of systems. Modularity is, also, a major feature in the development of programming languages and appears in the package construct of Ada. The interface to a component is defined and is visible to the users. The details of the component, what is on the inside, are not available, since the user does not need to know how it is done.

A new generation of applications is required to meet the business needs of the late 1990s. Client-server architecture, open systems and graphical-user interfaces are now able to offer cost-effective solutions for developing new systems.

To convert an existing information system into an open system one needs a strategic partner who understands the business and has the right expertise. A company developing open systems requires assurance from a supporting partnership.

The general open criteria and the areas where standardisation is expected, covers:

- operating systems. The language/s enabling the system to work,
- item-operability. The ability of two or more systems to exchange and use information,
- Relational Database Management Systems (RDBMS). Where the data are kept and the way these are sorted,
- project support,
- graphics language interfacing,
- multi-system interconnect,
- multi-processor Interconnect,
- portability. The ease with which an application, or hardware component can be transferred from one hardware or software environment to another,
- compatibility. Ability of two applications to co-ordinate with one another in their operation,
- re-usability. The ability to reuse portions of one application's software/hardware in the generation of another application,
- interfacing. The 'connection' to existing systems,
- maintainability. The qualities that improve the ability to maintain the application by eliminating interface uniqueness for parts of application code,
- performance.

The organisations and government departments as consumers of products, developed by others, needs guidance as to how to consider products. The term 'product' is used to denote, either a hardware product, a software product, or a combination of both. This can be called a 'consumer model':

- define system requirements,
- identify components and interfaces,
- select standards,

Andreas Sofroniou

- select implementations,
- integrate and test,
- deploy system,
- perform maintenance.

The international standard (ISO 9126), defines quality characteristics for products and guidelines for their use. The characteristics include:

- functionality,
- reliability,
- usability,
- efficiency,
- maintainability,
- portability.

Other groups have, also, defined quality attributes. The MITRE Guide to Software Quality is based on the following attributes:

- efficiency,
- reliability,
- maintainability,
- expandability,
- inter-operability,
- re-usability,
- integrity,
- survivability,
- correctness,
- verifiability,
- flexibility,
- portability.

The world is moving to open systems, components and modular architectures. The user must understand this world and be able to deal with it intelligently.

6.8   Superhighway

The chapter on COTS packages will not be complete without the inclusion of the communication and information derived from the 'superhighway'. The term itself is controversial. So is the concept of such a utility being part of COTS. On the other hand COTS can be utilised to bring into effect the management of information derived from or via the superhighway.

In the business world, a new kind of supporting infrastructure is necessary, because groups can only function properly when they can be supported by shared communications and applications.

The infrastructure of the new frontier is beginning to fall into place and, although the information superhighway is not open yet, the paths it will eventually follow are being laid now. The information superhighway is not a single communication method, or route. It is a combination of technologies and packages drawn from many different areas, which are converging to create a new global information infrastructure.

New type of software, such as 'groupware' have been designed to do just that. Equally, the development of tailored applications has been speeded up, either by a process of refinement to off-the-shelf applications, or by employing new development tools.

Not only are new products introduced faster, but new companies can come into existence as a result. The convergence of computers and telecommunications has already shown itself to be a powerful driving force in the economy. New technologies create new opportunities.

Andreas Sofroniou

THE MANAGEMENT OF COMMERCIAL COMPUTING

The premium on the management of information, not data, but information, is now huge. Often though, organisations have vast data resources, but make little real information available to those who might utilise it most. Often too, there is a flood of data, but little information.

The information superhighway is a complex, growing mesh of thousands of computer networks, joined together by a common computer language. It allows
the computer finally to realise its potential, with the seamless global exchange of text, superhighway represents a powerful tool with the potential to revolutionalise the way business is done.

Today's leading information highway is the Internet, a worldwide network of computers that has grown rapidly as more and more organisations recognise the value of sharing and exchanging information. The Internet works because it is based on the principles of open computing and networking, which allow many different types of computer to work together.

The Internet will deliver anything that can turn into digits. These days that includes text, graphics, voices, music, radio broadcasts, digitised photographs, art in general, formulae and moving video. When it is complete, the information superhighway will be the fastest route to the new frontier of an information based society.

All that is known for certain about the new technology, is that it will have much more powerful and cheaper computing. The Internet consists of computers and the cables that connect them and their users together. It must seem astonishing that such huge network has apparently grown up in a couple of years. In fact that is not how it happened. The Internet's roots go back 25 years through Arpanet, a network sponsored by the U.S. DoD.

The Internet already has over three million computers connected to it, in 146 countries. It is the requirements of the business world that are shaping the future of 'the Net'. The number of commercial users is growing at 92% a year, significantly faster than any other segment of the Internet user base. The technology required to gain access to the Internet today can consist of anything, from a laptop personal computer to a fully configured multi-user computer network.

The developments toward the information superhighway present the business community, government departments, educational establishments and individual users with unlimited opportunities for growth. The superhighway has the power potentially to revolutionise the way in which we communicate, educate, share information and conduct business.

The information superhighway will bring a range of services to businesses and the home. Despite the opportunities it offers, however, the information superhighway should be treated with care. The Internet used to be difficult to use and technologies must become more sophisticated and standards established before it can deliver its full potential. Security must be improved too, before the Net becomes a fully accepted trading channel.

The changeover to new ways of doing business, inevitably demands a heavy investment in staff training. With electronic mail increasingly taking the place of postal and facsimile services, administrative staff will have to become acquainted with more features on their personal computers, than just word processors and spreadsheets.

The European Union is committed to the creation of an information society. The recent 'Banggemann' report provides the basis upon which Europe's politicians will move forward. Progress in acting on their recommendations is slow. However, Europe is to build competitive advantage based upon the information revolution. Whereas the progress of Europe's political institutions is hampered by beaurocratic legislative processes, business leaders face no such obstacles.

The information superhighway has inspired many visions of the future, ranging from the utopian to the terrifying. The one clear message that comes from all the prophetic visions, however, is that the world will change radically. Successful 21st century businesses will be those that can adapt to the new electronic global infrastructure that the information superhighway will help to create.

The concept of a global 'macro-computer' evolving from the convergence of computers and telecommunications is not new. In the last 30 years, fiction has been augmented by more plausible, factually based predictions about the future impact of global computer networks. The emergence of the Internet as an early manifestation of the information superhighway allows us to see the shape of the future.

Andreas Sofroniou

The innovative services available on the Internet give us a clue to the marketplace of tomorrow and the demands it will place both on suppliers and consumers. Work still needs to be done to turn the Intrnet into a genuine information superhighway, but the structure is there. So, indeed, are the long term implications.

The issue of access security is attracting more attention as the commercial potential of the information superhighway is recognised. The government wants to see its operational data fully secured from unauthorised users. The availability of industrial-strength encryption techniques such as public key encryption is an important first step towards a fully secure environment.

The cause of security is further served by other technical innovations in software, especially the concept of object-oriented design. Objects can package data and process together in such a way that they are inaccessible to the user or other programs. This means, that information packages from the network can be examined safely without the fear of security breaches.

6.9   Modelling and Prototyping

Modelling is a theme usually associated with COTS integration. COTS as a prototyping tool can be used for Human-computer Integration (HCI) exercise mock-up. Once requirements are prototyped and agreed that the mock-up is representing what is needed, the prototyped development can be the start of the operational system.

The prototyping exercise can be based on a COTS package, which itself can interface with other COTS products. Prototyping can serve as system architecture where changes to needs can be inexpensive and the risks of development can be minimised. As in manufacturing procurement, prototyping will serve as a prompt for 'just-in-time' COTS products.

By prototyping, various COTS components can be 'glued' together to produce integrated systems. Many COTS products can serve as applications on a single computer, where all screen records can access and retrieve data for a COTS Relational Database Management System (RDBMS). At this co-operative level, COTS components know that other COTS exist for data exchange and transfer.

By integrating COTS at various levels, COTS components are submerged into larger applications, where they work together efficiently and transparently that they lose separate identities to end-user.

Many COTS products come with Application Programming Interfaces (API). With sets of procedures, functions, routines, or sub-routines which can be called from the application. Linked into application code, like any other routines, it is possible to build applications that simply call COTS APIs to produce desired functionality.

The proper way to acquire a COTS package for prototyping and modelling is to go through the exercise of collecting the requirements and subsequently, follow the various stages of development techniques and structured methodology.

The various stages of development as recommended and supported by the CCTA (The Central Computing and Telecommunications Agency, Millbank, London), are:

- current systems and requirements analysis,
- systems analysis, being the logical representation of the functions and requirements,
- systems designing, the detailed study of what the users want,
- package selection (if the COTS route is chosen),
- software testing,
- integration,
- user training.

In selecting a package, COTS requires evaluation on performance and inter-operability. Therefore, the following need to be checked:

- operating language/system,

- compilers,
- graphics software,
- project support environment,
- relational Database Management Systems,
- prototyping and the Human-computer interaction.

The increased use of COTS for prototyping is inevitable. So are the technologies and themes related to COTS integration.

COTS integration as a means to cut costs, is probably the premier motivation to use COTS. The cost reductions can be measured in the areas of shortened development schedules and cheap COTS software. The latter, in turn, ensures inter-operability and portability.

6.10   Review And Selection Of COTS

This section of the book serves as a draft guidance. It brings forward a methodology for the expansion of the study and suggests ways of approaching the selection of products by the users.

Currently, the available COTS studies are concerned with software, which can be purchased through the commercial, retail and wholesale distributors. Such procurements can include GOTS (Government Off-The-Shelf) and modified COTS (customised products).

The major point to be remembered is that COTS is a packaged product on which modification must be avoided. The COTS package in this case, will be used as is, in its intended format.

It is imperative that various checks are made prior to purchasing a COTS package. The initial enquiry will be based on the possible compatibility and interfacing of the package to the existing technical environment. As in every system development, the reliability, accuracy and security of the package is of importance.

The first draft will utilise information readily available. This, in turn, will prompt the necessary feedback from the reviewers. The comments and requirements received will be catalogued and incorporated in the COTS exercise.

Upon the receipt of comments and requirements, the study will encompass all aspects of computing. Within this subject, the choice of modules to be represented diagrammatically in a top-down structure, which will include all components of computing:
- system architecture,
- hardware,
- software,
- tools,
- implementation

Thus, COTS as a selection system, will assist in choosing the package appropriate to the following criteria:

- vendor independence, where competition will benefit economically,
- user productivity, through established consistency and predictability in services,
- reduced life-cycle cost, with minimum duplication of functionality,
- technology insertion. Stable vendor target paths for technology and modular insertion,
- scalability. Ability of applications to be configured,
- networking of hardware. Allow operations of platforms ranging from micros to mainframes.

Another goal that may be important, is the recognition that the use of COTS represents a shift in the way that systems will be built in the foreseeable future. If this is accepted by the Project Managers, then the users will want to:
- understand basic terms and concepts,
- recognise programmatic issues,

- recognise potential benefits of COTS and difficulties to be faced in creating systems based on COTS components,
- feel better equipped to deal with the requirements,
- recognise that there are no easy solutions. COTS systems are not the answer to everything.

6.11   COTS Advantages and Disadvantages

COTS Advantages

Avoidance of development costs
Use of established products
Latest, state-of-the-art
Shorter development cycle
More sources
Newer technology
Cheaper implementation
Easier interconnection
Technological advances as they occur.

COTS Disadvantages

Not tailored to specific applications
Entities (data) may not match
No control over future availability
No authority over latest version
May not be the product required
May change to meet demands of others
Vendor may stop supporting it
Discontinuation of a component

COTS will prove beneficial for the selection of small packages. It must be remembered that the bigger the system, less the chances for a shelf product. In the case of Open Systems, it may be beneficial to 'build' rather than to attempt to buy.

An advantage of COTS is the wide user base which helps expose problems and leads to products as an answer in a comparatively short time. Equally, obsolescence comes rapidly, which is hard to cope within the organisational culture used to long computing lifetimes.

The use of COTS is widely seen as a method of reducing costs. The reduction in costs is so sticking that all opportunities, where COTS can easily be applied, are vigorously pursued. The use of COTS is becoming extensive, but there are difficulties in extending COTS into combat and embedded systems deployed in war fighting roles.

The book is concerned with the use of COTS products in meeting operational information systems needs. There is already extensive use of COTS in strategic IS where the computer systems and the core operating software are fully commercial or based on commercial derivatives.

These trends are certain to continue as the capability of COTS to meet needs improves. Some of the constraints on COTS applications can be expected to diminish with time. The following are a few points :

- COTS producers sell packages for generic classes of users, not a single user,
- the consumer has no visibility into development or cost of COTS development,
- the evolution of software is driven by market forces,
- there will be compromising with requirements,
- COTS components may have no knowledge of each other.

Perhaps it is true that within many companies, the development of systems is always behind schedule and over cost, so why not make it someone else's problem? With this in mind, allow various vendors to compete with COTS offerings and through reduced duplication of functionality, meet the requirements.

Implementation of COTS architecture is probably the best method of reducing development time and system cost while using leading technology and improving compatibility between company departments and industry at large.

The integration of information appears to be the emerging goal in information management today. To achieve this, a realistic assessment of COTS is necessary and which level of the system architecture the COTS will satisfy. If information and information systems performance are critical to organisations, then a process for assessing emerging technology should be developed.

It is difficult to assess a COTS product line, but it is an important task. Such issues reflect the planning and accounting for the future. While the assessment of products has played an important role in determining the standards, standardisation on the products must be avoided.

The COTS system products provide a framework for the technical environment and vendor independence. Transition to the method of choosing the appropriate COTS based on the user requirements can be accomplished, but it needs skills to overcome the difficulties of the current business environment.

It must be remembered that COTS packages in their current development and evolution are not ready to cope with huge required systems, nor can they, just like that, replace the running systems. To replace existing operational systems and/or to develop new ones, based on user requirements, the proper development cycle must be followed.

This needs investigations into the current computer and manual systems, as a first step, followed by the analysis of the requirements, the documentation of both into a stage three logical design and then compare the modules of the new architecture with those offered by COTS packages.

COTS modules, in their present developmental state can only satisfy what the market at large needs. Tendencies towards information technology have always been individualistic. Perhaps a new culture needs to be nurtured. That of modifying the requirements to suit what is available in the COTS market.

Should the COTS route for systems be followed, the biggest obstacle will be the system training required by the users prior to running the COTS packages. Mistakes in industry have been made. One good example is that of an international company who went for a computer-aided manufacturing (CAM) package. The system was fine, but it nearly bankrupted this company and had to be rescued by other companies in the Group. The users of the CAM system were not prepared, or trained appropriately, to know how to operate the system.

It is stipulated that the larger the required system, the more difficult it will be for COTS to satisfy such needs. Modularising the architecture will help. It will be easier to select and compare COTS with sections of the required system.

Guidelines for the correct selection of COTS, its implementation and user training will have to be developed. For such a COTS selection system and guidelines to be developed, the System Architect must base this on what the users want. It is imperative, before proceeding with the guidelines, that comments and requirements are gathered and accordingly design the COTS selection package.

For the COTS selection system-to-be, this book suggests five major sections; System Architecture, Hardware, Software, Tools and Implementation. Each of these will be divided into various components which, in turn, will guide the Project Managers and other users in choosing the COTS package.

Such a guiding system for the selection of COTS packages has not been developed by anyone. Many are preparing standards and have a good idea of what they want, but guidelines as a system does not exist. Large organisations tend to work separately, therefore, very difficult to establish one common set of standards.

For small software needs, a COTS selection system can be implemented to suit all requirements. For large systems, perhaps a joint exercise will help. The know-how of the software houses and the experience of the commercial environment can be used in collaborative projects, which can include the concern with the software standards.

By the turn of the next millennium, it may be feasible (eventually), for COTS, the open systems and the standards that are associated with it, to assist in the integration of information technology and the sciences; computing, human behaviour and the specific sciences.

The diagram with the title 'Identify Customisation & Interface Needs Of Preferred Package', on the following page, incorporates four processes which may help the business in choosing an appropriate package.

1. In the first process, the business areas requiring the service are identified. The functions will include the study into the::
- timescales,
- interfaces,
- hardware,

- users' input.

2. In the second process, the vendor's features are identified. This needs the vendor's input for the:
- package features,
- costs,
- timescales,
- matching to users' requirements.

3. Process number three is used to match the package features to the business/users' requirements. This includes the:
- additional hardware required,
- any possible changes to the package features.

4. In this process, all the costs are added together. The total costs will include the charges for the:
- implementation,
- customisation,
- matching the final costs with those already agreed.

The diagram on next page shows the processes for the selection of packages (COTS). A DFD format has been used to show the simplicity in using diagrams.

7: Artificial Intelligence (AI)

7.1   Expert Systems

Until recently, computers have been concerned with handling numbers and data. Today, many fields of human endeavour express our ideas and problems in non-numeric (symbolic) terms. An Expert System is concerned with concepts and methods of symbolic inference and representation of knowledge. Special computer languages, principally LISP and Prolog, have been developed to process symbolic information. Computer programs written in these languages can be much shorter and clearer than their conventional equivalents. The penalty which is paid, is that on conventional computers the programs are much less efficient and a new generation of computers and languages have and still are being developed to improve their execution.

In October, 1981, the Japanese announced their intention to embark on a research programme to develop fifth generation computer systems. This programme, jointly undertaken by universities, independent institutes and major Japanese companies, aims to move the whole basis of computing from data to knowledge processing. What they hope to achieve, is simply the development of knowledge-based systems, which will be the future driving force of their economy.

Faced with this threat, most of the technologically advanced countries have launched vigorous research programmes of their own. In the U.S.A., both the public (via the Defense Research Projects Agency) and the private sector are investing heavily in artificial intelligence research tools.

The UK's response was the Alvey Programme, a collaborative research project involving academic and industrial effort. What all activity shows, is that the future of computing lies in Artificial Intelligence (AI) systems. Today, many products have computer systems as integral components; these systems can only benefit from artificial intelligence, so products with 'added AI value' will give a considerable market advantage to companies which produce them.

Many companies in the fields of defence, electronics, communications and manufacturing are already planning AI programs for this reason. In the financial sector, as well, market pressures will leave organisations with little choice. Without the power and versatility of AI, survival will be difficult.

The areas of expert systems is fashionable at the moment. Over the past fifteen years, interest in expert systems has increased dramatically, especially in the
commercial field. In practice, it must be understood that expert systems are not threatening traditional computer skills.

The objective in constructing an expert system is to program into the computer a representation of human knowledge. There is an area of controversy over what exactly constitutes the definition of an expert system. Basically, this rests on artificial intelligence, or computing science, to form the base on which such systems are founded. That is, whether the primary stress should be put on knowledge, or logic.

Expert systems deal with knowledge which is accepted and certified, rather than working at a point where new knowledge can then be refined and checked pragmatically, against a recognised specialist.

Problems occur where there is controversy over what constitutes knowledge. If statistics are involved, there can be more than one interpretation of any results of which are obtained.

The applications of expert systems are wider in scope, than mathematical techniques, because heuristics can be used in situations which are not precisely defined, such as decision making.

7.2   Applications Of Expert Systems

There has been steady growth in the commercial adoption of expert systems, although the number of firms employing them is still small, compared to the total number of companies using computers. Those organisations using these systems have been surprised at the progress that can be made in this area, if the requirements are not excessively ambitious at the outset. Companies that have introduced expert systems, have done so, not to replace the work of existing computer systems, but to add to the functions that can be done automatically for the firm.

Expert systems can be employed for a range of relatively simple operations, such as fault diagnosis, where they can marginally improve on the performance of the average fitter. Other areas of applications which are being currently used are for sales advice, customer order handling and some aspects of training.

Although such systems would benefit smaller firms, it is the larger companies which employ their own research groups and have larger budgets to accomplish the latest technical advances.

Much of the early development work was done through academic research. The business community has been particularly active in investigating knowledge communication systems, a branch of expert systems which concentrates on eliciting and distributing knowledge for human consumption other than using it for programming.

Research concentrates on defining that part of human knowledge and skill which passes on verbally, or is taken to be tacit knowledge by the practitioners. The technology is being used to write down, check and define this type of knowledge. In some cases, the resulting programs can be used for training purposes.

Applications of expert systems to medicine have already been given much publicity. Although there are not many systems in routine use, as yet. The potential of prototypes has been demonstrated and are now close to the flowering of expert systems as an aid to doctors and physicians.

There are limitations which are under investigation at the moment and it is clear that applications of this technology will continue to develop rapidly. Expert systems are potentially an extremely useful aid to many human activities, not least, because they aim to utilise nothing more elaborate than plain common sense.

7.3   The Short History Of Artificial Intelligence

Artificial Intelligence (AI) has been a recognised, although somewhat dispersed field of endeavour since the mid-fifties; the term 'expert system' is quite recent. Its main force for popularity is derived from two major sources. First, the recognised inflexibility of established commercial computing and second, the promise given by new insight that intelligent machine behaviour could be achieved. The solution proposed to eliminate many evolving difficulties, is to refocus attention on the 'knowledge', rather than the 'data'.

Among the outstanding problems of knowledge engineering and expert systems development, are those relating to the difficulty of transferring their 'knowledge' from the human expert to the machine. It has been suggested, that one solution to the difficulty, lies in the use of inductive method for transfer, which would allow the expert to input examples from which the program can infer the rules, i.e. the inductive method should allow some automation of the knowledge engineer's task.

The resulting expert system must, of course, conform to the:

- agreed expert systems requirements,
- extend over a reasonable domain of expertise,
- give reliable decisions,
- its 'reasoning' must be accessible, both for the expert and non-expert user.

A further constraint, could require the expert system to deliver new knowledge, recognisable by the human expert, as such.

When faced with a complex task, the experienced programmer splits it into sub-problems. Each sub-problem is then programmed as a procedure and procedures can be nested to any level. The precise choice and hierarchical order of sub-problem in the province of top-down design is called 'structured induction'.

7.4   The Fifth Generation Language

The next generation of computer systems - the fifth generation language (5GL) - seeks to develop artificial intelligence (AI), which will greatly expand the applicability of computer systems from data processing into knowledge processing.

Since the fifties, computer researchers have believed that it is possible to make computers which can, to a limited extend, be considered to be capable of reasoning. The technical problems are enormous and it is only the last ten years, or so, that commercial organisations have begun to exploit artificial intelligence technology.

In its simplest form, artificial intelligence represents the ability of a computer to encompass the knowledge and problem-solving skills of experts from a range of disciplines; it helps the computer user to interpret information from several viewpoints, presenting that information in a form which allow a well informed decision about a particular problem to be made.

7.5   Techniques

Artificial intelligence techniques play a major part in improving the interface between humans and computers - image and speech understanding and robotics have all benefited from AI research.

By the end of the year 2000, it is forecast that more than thirty percent of existing computer applications will use artificial intelligence techniques and an even greater volume of new applications of computers will have arisen, addressing complex problems, which cannot currently be solved using today's computers.

Many of the world's largest companies are already developing AI-based applications. These are frequently called 'expert', or 'knowledge-based' systems. They seek to assist, or even replace 'experts', thus releasing manpower for more creative tasks.

To develop these complex systems quickly and efficiently, a new type of computer is needed. This is because the computer language normally used for AI applications requires much more processing power, than most conventional computers and more importantly, the computer power is used in a different way.

The principal difficulty lay in the fact that the fifth generation languages, which are most suitable for AI applications are very processor intensive and require novel computer architectures for efficient execution. Since commercial AI applications need, almost without exception, to interact with 'conventional' data processing systems, this imposes a serious limitation in their use. One solution is to network these 'machines' to a more general purpose computer.

7.6   Meeting The Needs Of Industry

Applying artificial intelligence techniques to industrial applications is not very easy. Some of the most useful AI-based solutions, such as continuous speech recognition, will not be practicable until later in the decade. However, a number of useful applications have already been developed to the extend that they show a substantial commercial benefit. The most commonly discussed application is the expert system.

The expert system seeks to encapsulate the knowledge and skills of highly qualified individuals (usually a scarce resource) and increase productivity by applying these skills equally and consistently throughout the organisation. Expert systems are particularly applicable where the task is repetitive, but low level. For example, configuring large computer systems is a good application for an expert system, but designing computers is not.

One of the most frequent mistakes which is made in designing expert systems is to under-estimate the size of the knowledge base which is required.

The major use of expert systems is for the rapid prototyping and development of complex software systems. Programmer productivity using the window-oriented graphics work-station and the high level software tools shows a ten-fold productivity increase over conventional programming language on a good quality super-personal computer.

Although 5GLs are generally associated with symbolic computing, many AI applications, also, require good performance for non-symbolic processing. Image-processing, model-based expert systems and systems accessing conventional databases are some examples.

In recent years, shell-based application packages have increased in many areas of systems. As a result, many companies explain how they have been using shells as tools to create complete 'virtual' models of their products and manufacturing processes and the benefits in cost, money and quality that shells have given them.

The installation of CAD\CAM\CAE\CASE technology, within a framework of concurrent engineering, has resulted in improvements in the design-to-manufacture lead-times for the producers of goods at large. The world of manufacturing and computing technology continues to advance at breakneck speed and keeping up can be difficult for those technology is intended. This year has seen the launch of numerous new products for expert systems in engineering.

8: CASE Tools And Methodologies

8.1   The Overall Objectives

As organisations strive to increase productivity, to reduce costs, to shorten cycle times, to improve product and service quality, so the demands made on systems for modifications and for new information increase. Being able to make better decisions based on quality information and having the flexibility to respond to new opportunities increasingly, depends on having the right systems in place at the right time.

Applications developed based on older technologies may well not meet current requirements in some or many areas, such as:
- functionality,
- ease of use,
- data access,
- maintainability,
- flexibility,
- robustness,
- costs.

With the wide range of application environments and building blocks now available, it is still possible to have an affordable system designed and built to meet specific business requirements. This gives the flexibility and control to define the system the way the users want it and then to change and adapt the system to support the business over coming years.

Computer-aided Software Engineering (CASE) tools address the application design stage. For business systems they can be extremely useful to assist in the design of both, the application and the data structure.

Rapid Application Development (RAD) techniques incorporate a series of steps which business people and Information Technology professionals work through together to develop a prototype of the application representing the business process before full scale development.

The objectives of analysis is to understand what a particular area of the business does and how information is exchanged, created and modified by business processes.

With a clear understanding of the information needs of a business area, the system engineer can determine which business activities to automate and then develop those systems so they meet end user requirements.

The design helps users move from a logical representation of 'what' a given system is to perform, into the physical specifications for 'how' the system will actually be implemented.

In order to handle the complex nature of a system, it is often helpful to break down the processes and data of the system into manageable pieces. Decomposition diagrams are an easy way to partition the data and process requirements of the system, by analysing and application, refining high level business processes into lower level processes. These processes can then be broken down further until the analyst reaches a level of detail where a process can best be described in terms of its procedural logic.

The decomposition diagram helps to create and maintain diagrams for :

- process decomposition; depict the analysis of processes into subprocesses,
- data decomposition; show how general groupings of data break down into more specific data entities,
- organisational decomposition; describe the hierarchical structure of the organisation.

The analysis stage is unique in its approach to integrating the process model with the data model. The analyst can build the application data model by defining, one at a time, the data model for each individual process.

Dataflow diagrams can help describe how a business area or system functions. They show how data flows into and out of the business area or system, how processes transform data and the external agents (recipients/sources) that interface with the system.

Entities are the subjects of information (people, places, things) about which a business needs to keep data. An entity diagram provides a graphic way of describing the data requirements of a system and how they interrelate. The entity diagram, also, helps describe and characterise the relationships among these entities.

In many Information Technology (IT) departments, the complexity of applications often dictates that development responsibilities be divided among members of a project team. The ability to share information is a fundamental requirement for systems development tools.

Such tools, Computer-aided Software Engineer (CASE - some system engineers describe them as 'System', instead of 'Software') tools are designed to offer unequalled flexibility in combining and reconciling the work of multiple users. The analyst can selectively consolidate and separate, either whole, or partial encyclopaedias, or selected objects and maintain multiple encyclopaedias for different projects or users.

8.2   The CASE Tool And The Encyclopaedia

For an IT department to be a valued contributor to the company's success, its staff must be supplied with tools to respond effectively to business opportunities, where CASE tools can assist in the full life cycle of the applications development.

Applications which reduce costs and add value, effectiveness. For IT to be a valued contributor in business, its functions and service to users must be highly adaptive, in planning, manufacturing, products design, marketing and the overall company culture. To succeed in such concepts, IT conducts an inter-departmental analysis of its information systems, to assess its assets and capabilities.

Based on the investigation, the IT department may recommend COTS packages as a solution to the applications demand made by the company, or IT may recommend systems developed internally.

Whichever the choice, new concepts and advanced technologies will be introduced to the organisation. These cost money, but properly approached, the IT will be able to design new systems, or apply COTS packages in a much easier and less costly way.

As part of the new concepts, IT will bring forward a long range strategic plan for business systems. Evolve from a business system planning to an overall technical architecture planning approach. Tools, including CASE, are the key to the success of the overall technical architecture.

From the user perspective, the analysis of problems is critical. Detailed analyses of the operating systems, the manual systems and the functional relationships will serve the purpose of the overall architecture. A CASE tool is highly instrumental, in being able to present the numerous applications to management and users and to gain consensus among the staff..

One of the strengths of the CASE tool is its ability to hold information,
definitions and comments. With a user-friendly tool, the analyst finds it easier to start and modify the diagrams. The users understands what the IT is doing. Pictures generated out of the tool are shown to the users for consensus and where necessary the diagrams get back into the tool to redraw.

The tool makes it easy. Diagrams are redrawn quickly and using the tool causes the analysts and users to question the analysis more. The result is a better quality system.

The CASE tool will prompt the analyst to begin with a decomposition of the areas that are involved and then a global data model which can be used as the starting point for the data model side of the project. These are explained to the users. In doing so, the design tool makes things easier. The analyst can move things around on the screen, which encourages modular design techniques.

As explained, the IT project team is responsible for the research and development of the advanced concepts and technologies in support of the company's information systems. The IT is not only responsible for the traditional data administration duties, but also for the introduction of the CASE tools and the building up of the encyclopaedia.

The successful introduction of the CASE tool and its encyclopaedia the following are strongly recommended:
- standardisation of methodology throughout the organisation,
- substantial investment in training IT staff and users,
- pilot the overall technical architecture.

It is fair to say that until recently, software development was more art than science. Applications were implemented in an undisciplined manual process that seemed to take for ever. Application backlogs got worse instead of improving.

Today, applications can be engineered and with the assistance of vendors and their products, applications are constructed to suit the users within realistic timescales. Users of CASE tools should develop better systems in less time.

CASE tools are used for planning, analysis, design and allow for the capturing of the user system requirements. All the specifications as diagrams and descriptions. Following on, application generators can then process these pictures to create complete applications for most environments.

If the application has been fully specified, this will include the source code, plus database definitions, the database access routines, screen maps and system level documentation. In short, everything a system engineer needs to compile and test the application.

Some vendors offer CASE tools which are tied to a specific methodology. This means that the system to be developed will be the vendor's way, no matter what the type, size, or scope of the project. A good CASE tool should not be constrained to a specific methodology.

Some CASE tools on the market are:
- IEF,
- IEW,
- Excelerator,
- LBMS System Engineer,
- Select, etc.

The IT should be free to choose and use any of these methodologies:
- James Martin's Information Engineering,
- Yourdon,
- DeMarco,
- Gane and Sarson,
- Arthur Young,
- Constantine,
- War-Mellor,
- BIS Modus,
- LSDM,
- SSADM,
- Prototyping, etc.

The application development lifecycle is common to almost all established methodologies and is often broken down into four major phases:
- planning,
- analysis,
- design,
- construction.

Andreas Sofroniou

Developers will typically invest the most time in the first three phases. This emphasis on the front-end assures that the application being developed will be the right one and that it will be constructed the right way.

In the three front-end phases, relationships and system requirement specifications are most clearly and concisely represented as diagrams. In the back-end construction phase, a good CASE tool offers application generator solutions that can transform pictures into working systems.

One of the secrets to the success of the good CASE tool is the encyclopaedia and the consistency through it. The CASE tools with one common encyclopaedia ensure that the data are shared and that the diagrams and their meanings are always consistent with each other.

Each time a diagram is requested, the expert system within the CASE tool automatically generates it from knowledge contained in the encyclopaedia. Likewise, each time information is entered, the encyclopaedia interprets the meaning and can represent it in many different diagram forms.

As the content of the encyclopaedia is updated, the tools automatically update all the diagrams that are affected by the change. So there is no need for manually auditing the consistency among diagrams for every revision.

When system engineers are drawing diagrams on paper, it is not easy to see how all the parts of a large application will come together. As a result, diagrams may be missing inputs, relationships, or outputs that go nowhere.

CASE tools automatically guide the analyst through fundamental principles that are common to all methodologies. The CASE tool calls attention to errors, inconsistencies and checks for completeness. This automatically assures that the systems requirement specifications and designs created with the tool, can be transformed into real systems.

As has already been seen, the CASE tools include PC-based diagramming tools and application generators, all driven from a common encyclopaedia. The encyclopaedia is, also, the key to integrating the work of planning, analysis and design. Information captured with analysis is also available to the design phase and vice versa. This way the work of one phase can become the foundation for work in the next phase. Changes made during design will be reflected automatically back to the analysis diagrams.

By capturing all of the details in a single encyclopaedia the analyst can develop a shared resource of integrated information. This will be based on the user's needs. It will support the entire system specification and the system lifecycle. It will, also, have all the details needed to generate applications and databases. This way the systems can be maintained at the design level instead of at the coding stage.

If the IT has more than one person on a project, or multiple of modules or projects going on simultaneously, the CASE tool and its common encyclopaedia allows this automatically, while preserving the integrity of the diagrams and the knowledge they represent. The CASE tool combines the encyclopaedias, removes all redundancies and detects all potential conflicts and discrepancies.

The CASE tools use the latest user interface and are mouse-driven, with full windowing capabilities. The screens let the user point at commands, instead of remembering what the commands are and when they are to be used.

Several diagrams can be displayed on the screen at one time. This lets the user see the flow of information from one diagram to the next. Because diagrams are so easy to create and modify, analysts are more willing to exchange ideas with end-users and explore alternative paths to the best solution of the problems and the requirements.

CASE tools are a fairly new technology and systems engineers are still finding many ways to implement the potentials offered. Some CASE tools are design to be modular with separate tools for planning, analysis, design and application generation. These tools can work together as a single integrated product, or separately as individual ones.

To be practical, a CASE tool must be able to work with many other packages. These should include such things as:
- data dictionaries,
- databases,
- 4GLs,

- standard repositories,
- code generators,
- software testing platforms,
- compilers
- purchased COTS applications.

At the end of the day, no matter what anyone may say, a CASE tool, or any product may fail the IT department and the business as a whole, unless a properly documented system requirements specification is produced. A specification upon which everything will depend - to deliver what the user asked.

9: Systems Specification

9.1 The Highlights Of The Case Study

The documentation of the system requirements specification is concerned with the overall definition of the recommended system and the production of the required system, following the selection from the business systems options.

This stage of the project delivers the:

- functional decomposition (hierarchical diagram),
- processes (dataflow diagrams),
- data structure (model and relationships),
- data inventory,
- functions, transactions, events,
- requirements catalogue,
- problems solved,
- menus and screen reports,
- associations of all above,
- definitions of all above,
- activity plan (with the steps for each phase of development).

The case study presented in this chapter, is that of an imaginary retailer specialising in the selling of products through branches. The study incorporates logistics ideas as part of the electronic point-of-sale overall architecture. The fictional study shown in the following pages, is just one module of an overall retailing system. The company has inventories in warehouses as well as in the branches.

This exercise will look into the function of recalled goods by suppliers/manufacturers and how the branches return the recalled stocks. The specification will include the returning of excessive stocks from the branches to the designated company warehouses. The requirements, also, cover cases where goods need to be transferred from branch to branch.

The diagrammatic representations, descriptions and associations were produced by the LBMS System Engineer. This CASE tool can easily accommodate the methodologies of LSDM and the British government preferred SSADM. In order to illustrate the similarities of the many methodologies on the market, the study tried to cover many concepts of as many methodologies as possible.

This exercise deals with the excessive stock of products within the 'company' (and its 'branches') and the attempt to reduce the stockroom size.

The ordering algorithm to improve the re-ordering of stock to the branches is already established within the purchasing practices. Overstocks occur and unwanted goods still need to be returned to manufacturers and own warehouses. Further on, stocks have to be redeployed, by transferring the goods to other branches.

Due to the inability of the current systems, to cope with the demand made upon them, the company is losing quarter of all reclaimable moneys from recallable items.

The main problems of the current systems are, the:

- branch being unable to complete the returns any quicker,
- speed of goods travelling through the supply chain,
- timescales of goods being sorted and credit requested.

The implementation of this module will enable the substantial reduction stockroom space and savings in cashflow.

The major processes of this module, include:

- the receiving of instructions to return goods; which details can be generated by the external recipient/sources Centre (Head Office), Supplier, Area Manager, or another Branch,
- the Branch seeking authorisation to return unwanted stock,
- following the instructions to return or transfer, the Branch selects the products listed,
- the dispatching of items from the Branch to the Warehouse, or Supplier,
- following the dispatch of stock, the Branch verifies the credits and debits allocated by the Centre.

The data model subset represents nine major entities, which hold the appropriate attributes.
The entities involved are:

- Recall,
- Return,
- Inter-branch Transfer,
- Item,
- Stock Adjustment,
- Branch,
- Supplier,
- Warehouse,
- Claim.

Other aspect for consideration, regarding the specification of this module are:

- The Problems and Requirements Catalogue of the current fictional systems holds requirements applicable to the development of this module.
- The solutions to every problem listed has been found, agreed by the users and accordingly, the necessary associations to the CASE objects have been made.
- The fictional people who may participate in the production of the imaginary required system, are the members of the users consultative committee, the Head Offices (Centre) staff and representatives from the branches.

Additionally, there are a number of constraints which the senior management need to make a decision; company policies and methods of working.

Some of the issues are:

- different types of instructions procedures,
- various types of returns,
- different sets of delivery standards,
- inaccurate collation of the recalled products,
- other topics which involve a number of different departments.

In this case the users consultative committee, chaired by a senior manager, undertakes to resolve the issues, outside the scope of this system specification.

9.2   The Diagrammatic Representation

By now, all the phases, starting from the Project Initiation Document (PID), right through to the required analysis, the users problems and requirements cataloguing, their solutions and the specification of the required system, all are complete. The next step, is for the users to sign off this phase of the module, prior to starting on the building of the system.

The reader will appreciate that the volume of the documentation of the complete study of this fictional module may consist of more than one thousand pages. In view of this, only a few examples are selected as extracts of the system requirement specification. The full documentation of a module such as the example presented usually takes a small team of people a few months to complete.

Therefore, only one example of each one of the following is included in this book:

- Functional Decomposition Diagram and Report,
- Data Model Subset Diagram and Components,
- Data Inventory,
- Dataflow Diagrams Set and Descriptions,
- Functions,
- Transactions,
- Events,
- Problems and Requirements Catalogue,
- Solutions,
- Menu And Screens Reports.

Once all above are inserted in the CASE tool, the automatic outputs, included in the specifications, individually show the listing of all the components, within each picture, with the appropriate descriptions for each component. Everyone of the components are associated to each other. Examples of the CASE tool outputs are shown on the following pages:

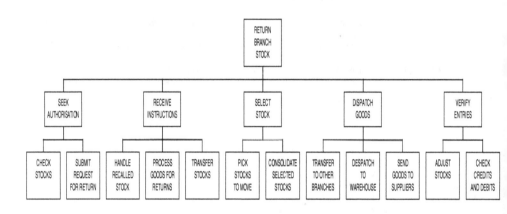

10: Information Systems Explained

10.1   Information Systems Now

It is hard to imagine business today without information systems. Information Technology in general is an important part of business and everyday life. It has become very important for individuals and organisations, in the ability to compete, perform and prosper.

As a support structure and as a tool for business, systems can deliver a number of significant benefits. Costs can be reduced, productivity increased, services improved and profits enhanced.

People at the sharp end of business, want a better understanding of the way that systems are developed and function. It is hoped that in this book systems issues are explained and that computing helps people to comprehend the broad aspects of technologies available to assist in achieving personal and business objectives.

Systems ought to be about enabling business and personal change.

10.2   Commerce And The Internet

The term 'Electronic Commerce' is commonly used to mean doing business electronically. It is the paperless exchange of critical business information between companies and their suppliers, government departments, financial institutions, customers and companies, even within organisations.

Business today see the electronic commerce as a way to streamline operations, reach new markets and serve their clients more efficiently. It can often be a catalyst for business change through business process re-engineering. A streamlined new process nearly always entails some degree of automation. Since many business processes cut across boundaries between departments, divisions and even companies, electronic commerce is a natural way to automate these processes.

A popular method of communication for exchanging data is Electronic Data Interchange (EDI). EDI may be defined as the 'exchange of standardised structured information between computer systems'.

EDI lends itself to the exchange of high volumes of information in a fixed format agreed by industry groups. This includes invoicing and payments, retail point-of-sale, bank transactions and manufacturing inventories. Because information is created and transferred electronically, there is no need for paperwork. This eliminated the need for re-keying data, which saves labour, speeds up processes and reduces details errors. Significant cost savings and reduced lead times can be achieved.

Processes can be automated and re-structured so that maximum operational efficiency is obtained. EDI operates by direct connection between users and over private and public data networks, ensuring privacy and security. As it uses highly structured formats, transmission speeds can be increased and overall costs reduced.

An electronic commerce business solution relies on a network to act as a conduit for the transfer of data. Often, a 'value-added network' from a commercial provider is used, to provide the infrastructure required to transfer data securely and reliably among trading partners.

One of the ideas brought forward, is whether the Internet will replace these value-added network services. The Internet is one methods of exchanging business data, but not the only means. A commercial network eliminates many of the technical matching issues and provides services not available on the Internet, such as security, tracking and audit ability. The Internet is an important element of an electronic commerce solution, but is not the only one.

10.3   Internet In Business

Until a few years ago, the Internet was not well known. One could scarcely have predicted the impact it would have on the world of systems and computers communications.

From its inception in the 1960s, the Internet evolved into a global network of business, academic and government computers. In recent years, businesses and individual users have recognised its potential as a way of communicating. By exchanging electronic mail, transferring files, accessing information services and communicating via bulletin boards and computer conferencing.

The communication has been accompanied by the emergence of a part of the Internet known as the World Wide Web, which allows information to be presented in a graphical format; incorporating text, images, video and sound. Any user with a suitable personal computer can access the Web through a connection to the Internet using the normal telephone line and view information using low cost software tools, known as browsers.

Businesses are now setting up electronic shop-fronts and information sites on the World Wide Web and starting to realise the immense potential for reaching a global audience.

However, this open access to the vast storehouse of information raises a number of issues. The openness of the Internet leads to concerns over security. The Internet is a public set of networks that interconnect and are not inherently secure. As a consequence, there is a demand for effective software security tools known as 'firewalls'. These act as a secure gateway to limit outsiders' access to a company's data systems and provide control over staff access to the Internet.

Companies and individuals are reluctant to transmit and exchange sensitive details over the Internet, such as credit card information. The problem is now being addressed by developing effective encryption tools. The combination of firewalls and encryption will enable the realisation of the Internet's full commercial potential.

One genuine limiting factor on Internet usage is data transmission speeds. Although these have improved in recent years, for most users they remain painfully slow. It takes a few minutes to download and read even a basic Web page. Transferring large data files is often impractically slow. These and other management issues associated with security, training and implementation, should be taken into account when considering the Internet as part of a business strategy.

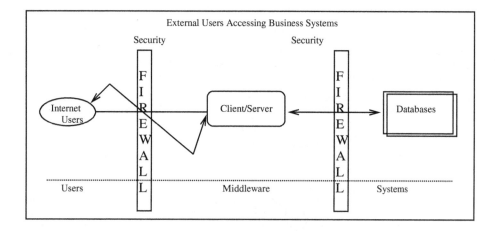

10.4   The Mainframe

Over the years, the word was that the mainframe computer was on the way out. The growth of the personal computers on the desk-top was claimed to replace the mainframe as the preferred business information technology platform, well before the end of the century.

The reports of the mainframe's death have turned out to be greatly exaggerated. The fact that mainframes have been around for so long helps explain why companies still use them.

Historically, data has been safe and secure on a mainframe. The cost and benefits of moving it to another type of system are difficult to justify. The longevity of the mainframe means that it is a mature environment as far as security, structure and disciplined operational processes are concerned. Innovations in computing may appear to be more sophisticated, but lack the tools to deliver the integrity, security and availability of data required to run critical business systems.

Mainframes are still perceived to be the best place for sensitive information and for running data intensive centralised systems, such as personnel, payroll, accounts and inventories.

10.5   The Mainframe As A Data Server.

In modern computing environments, the mainframe assumes a new role. Additional to its running of large systems, it is becoming a large-scale data server. Companies recognise the need to provide centralised management and protection for critical data distributed throughout the organisation. In fact, the amount of data storage on the mainframe is growing and so is the data held on systems elsewhere. This gives the systems function the added responsibility of storing, organising, managing and distributing the data.

The concept of managing data across an organisation requires the facility to manage its storage in a uniform manner, implementing consistent policies and standards and enforcing the protection of critical data. This is achieved via the use of software tools, which offer an overall view of the data stored.

The concept of storage management is well established in the mainframe environment and has been the basis for the replication of those disciplines across the business enterprise, leading to more efficient use of resources, greater ease of management and security of information.

10.6   The Use Of PCs And Mainframes

Desk-top personal computers have become extensively used alongside mainframes. The emergence of the PC led to a different perception of computing. Users expect systems which are easy to build, operate and use, with highly graphical and intuitive screens. These facilities have not been a strength of the mainframe in the past.

Many organisations have rationalised a requirement for centralised control with the need for end user autonomy by creating links and networks, utilising the strengths of both mainframes and personal computers. In effect, the mainframe is used to collect, store and process business information from a variety of sources, with individuals and work groups then accessing the centralised data using PCs.

Software houses have risen to this challenge by developing a range of software tools which allow PC users to access and analyse mainframe data and integrate it with desktop systems, such as spreadsheets, word processors and other business software tools. They need to be able to locate relevant information easily, using everyday PC language rather than specialised computer commands and are not interested in where the information lies and how it is retrieved.

The users expect to be able to search all available data sources in one go without worrying about the different structures and systems used by the various databases they are searching. Alternatively, links can be created between the PC and mainframe applications enabling automatic update of desk-top data whenever the source is changed on the mainframe.

10.7 The Mainframe For Management Services

The longevity of the mainframe means that the management of services it provides to the business is well understood and consequently more controllable. The mainframe acts as a hub, linked to many other areas of the organisation's systems and provides a central viewpoint for ensuring that users have systems up and running when they need them.

Consequently, a range of tools to manage the operational side of providing these services has evolved. These allow a high degree of automation and relate the services to their importance to the business. Hence, if a part of the system, or network fails, the services which are most critical to the running of the business can be addressed first, whilst less critical services assume a lower priority. In today's business environment, when organisations trade round the clock, management of systems to this sophistication is vital to business success. This type of service, simply cannot be managed without the control available with mainframe systems.

The mainframe plays an important part of the evolution of an organisation's systems and often provides the most logical platform to run business systems effectively. If the mainframe did ever die, it has certainly risen again.

10.8 The Client Server

A client/server system is a 'modular' approach to computer systems. Instead of all aspects of the system being held in one place, a server holds applications and data which can be accessed from a number of 'clients' who have their own processing capability.

In the most advanced systems, any computer on the network could act as a server for some applications and as a client for others. This is significantly different to the conventional local area network (LAN), where typically one computer will control the network and hold data, although applications tend to be held on each PC or workstation.

Client/server systems were conceived when the personal computer emerged as a credible platform for business systems. Users became accustomed to powerful desk-top applications and the ease of use provided by graphical user interfaces, such as Windows and OS/2. By linking these computers, it was reasoned, mainframe-based business systems could be replaced with groups of computers which were collectively as powerful, but individually easier and more flexible to use.

10.9 Flexibility To The Users

The new-style systems support greater integration and collaboration between corporate-wide and single user desk-top applications. Employees at all levels of an organisation have access to a company's systems, but do not need the support and training associated with traditional text-based programs. This wider use of graphical interfaces across the enterprise has enabled the implementation of better reporting tools and more flexible access to data through sophisticated information systems.

One of the reasons for the evolution of the client/server philosophy was the growth of power on the desk-top, via the personal computer. However, organisations soon realised that a huge amount of data resided elsewhere in the business, often collected and collated over many years and held in a secure and controlled environment, such as mainframe computers. There seemed to be little reason to migrate or relocate these systems on to a different type of computer, especially if the underlying business processes they would support were to remain fundamentally the same.

For this reason, the client/server concept encompasses all sizes of computers and not just the PC. However, a business structures its systems and data, the most important business benefit to be delivered is increased ease of use and flexibility of data access. Often, the best returns on investment in client/server have been achieved when personal computers have provided an interface with existing systems, but with the retention of the underlying programs and processes.

When implementing client/server systems, organisations can, therefore, choose between developing simple graphical interfaces to enable a personal computer to access mainframe data, or they may decide on a totally new application built from scratch. In each case, effective software tools are needed to develop the new interfaces and support the integration of new and old systems.

10.10   Tools For Effective Systems

Software tools are available which cover virtually every aspect of building and implementing client/server systems. The best are easy to use, typically running on PCs. Structurally incorporating rapid application development concepts and processes which involve the input of business users into the building of effective systems to support business needs. Usually, tools of varying kinds are required to make the most of computing elements already in existence.

Systems re-engineering software enables existing mainframe applications to be transferred to other computer types without losing the original investment in programming. Connectivity tools and terminal emulation software enable computers to access information on different platforms. Graphical development tools assist users to create new screen layouts and applications. Alternatively, fast productivity gains can be achieved from the use of integrating software, which takes older-style, text-based applications and creates an easy to use graphical screen for the user. Not only is this easier to use and, therefore, more productive, but it means that a number of applications can be combined on the desk-top.

Users of the systems need access to data wherever it is located, without having to be concerned with where it is, or techniques of accessing it. Sophisticated software tools are available to locate data stored in multiple locations and to allow it to be extracted in a common format for compilation of reports and integration into other applications.

It would be true to say that, in many organisations, client/server is happening
despite IT and not because of it. The amount of technology and skill accumulating on the desk-top is growing exponentially , as is the need to connect to shared resources such as databases and mail services. A move to client/server should deliver concrete business advantages, integrating the PC and the corporate mainframe, thus increasing flexibility.

Such corporate integration leads to more direct business involvement in the use of information technology. However, there is often increased cost associated with client/server over a traditional centralised computing structure. A complete realignment of the IT function is needed to provide managed support to the distributed systems which are now running the business.

10.11   Inherited Systems

Most organisations have an inherited legacy of systems. These inherited systems will have been in operation for a number of years, on mainframes and running bespoke systems which were written in house, or by a contracting consultant. At first sight, legacy systems appear to have limited use in a modern organisation, with the exception of one very important fact. Their longevity means they hold a huge amount of vital, critical data. The business processes which they support, have been developed over the years and investment made in getting the systems right.

With the industry hype on the demise of the mainframe, organisations started to wonder whether the mainframe and the legacy systems running on it were declining and whether they should be replaced with new workstation and client/server systems. However, reality shows that this vast change is not easily achieved, that companies still depend upon legacy systems for the vast majority of their operations and that new systems continue to be built for the mainframe.

It has transpired that most of the conflict between the new client/server technologies and legacy applications is based on misconceptions. Companies can gain significant advantages by incorporating new features into legacy systems. Re-use of legacy code significantly reduces cost and risk, while spending the time taken to deliver new business systems.

Sophisticated software tools enable IT departments to inspect, assess, document and record their legacy applications scientifically and objectively. Further tools can then be used, if required, to extract the best of the application code and provide the basis for migration to new developments.

Since legacy systems may have been constantly developed over the years, it is also important to use the relevant software tools to re-document their structure, to ensure that they can be supported and maintained. This ensures that the vital business processes they support are not threatened.

One current issue requiring this attention is the 'Year 2000' issue. Many legacy systems were envisaged to have a short life and needed to minimise the use of computer storage which was relatively expensive in the early days of systems building. These systems were written to hold only last two digits of the year in the date field and have endured and played a vital role in running the business.

It is now necessary to use appropriate software tools to identify all occurrences of 2-digit fields and change them to 4-digit, otherwise systems will assume that the date is reset to 1900, when the new millennium is reached. An example of this would be a financial loan application, which would mature before it started, interest due would be impossible to calculate and chaos would reign.

The typical computer user today needs to access and use information throughout the organisation to produce business plans, reports and presentations. The users need to draw information from a variety of sources to help them make the sort of high quality informed decisions that give their business competitive edge, greater efficiency and improved productivity.

Many organisations have realised that their legacy systems can have a prolonged life if the information they hold can be made available to this new type of user. For this reason, legacy systems are often incorporated into client/server systems, where PC users have direct, but controlled access to mainframe data.

In these situations the mainframe is used as a secure gateway to corporate mission-critical systems and as a centralised repository for enterprise data. As an example, retailers and financial institutions are continuing to use legacy systems to control most of their on-line transactions for hole-in-the-wall cash machines, or electronic point-of-sale data collection and processing.

With this new understanding of legacy systems and the tools that now exist to leverage their potential, their future is assured. Legacy systems can be integrated effectively with new systems, so that the data they hold and business functions they support are available throughout the enterprise. This not only prolongs their cost-effective life but also reduces costs through minimising the need to acquire new skills and purchase new hardware, software and infrastructure.

10.12   Data Warehousing

In this 'information age', making the best possible use of data is one of the biggest challenge facing the international organisation.

Historically, companies have acquired and managed data using separate computer systems for each application, with each optimised for its particular use. For this reason, data relating to sales, inventory, financial controls, customer service, personnel and other parts of the organisation is often held in a variety of locations and formats. Where links do exist among different applications, they often identify connections, or relationships between two different pieces of data. For example, linking a sale to a payment received.

While understanding this data is important, businesses need to make analyses in more complex ways. Managers and executives need to be able to make informed judgements and effective decisions in order to keep their business competitive, efficient and profitable.

This requirement is addressed by the an executive information system (EIS). Designed to help managers perform their responsibilities better, this system allows them to assess current and future business requirements by providing sophisticated analytical tools, such as trends analysis and what-if scenarios.

Because EIS enables effective decision making based on higher quality data, it is often classified as a business intelligence system (BIS), decision support systems (DSS), or management information system (MIS). While this may be true, it does not mean that these terms apply exclusively to EIS. They are, in fact, more often used to describe generic business information systems, while EIS has a more precise meaning.

If data from a variety of sources is placed in a central repository, it can all be accessed and analysed by an information system at the same time. This concept is known as a data warehouse. The key strength of data warehousing is the information advantage. All businesses, especially service businesses, want to know more about their customers. Data warehousing technology gives users instant access to data about all aspects of the company's business, without having to re-write applications to find it.

The data warehousing concept started out on the mainframe. The aim was to build large databases of historical information that could be extensively analysed, without affecting the performance of production systems. On a smaller
scale, companies also built multiple management information systems, but they did not pull together data from across the enterprise and many were built using conventional tools which made them difficult for unskilled users.

The data warehouse addresses the IT department's need to manage data that, with the rise of client/server distributed computing, is now dispersed across different platforms and is in varied and often incompatible forms. The arrival of new technologies such as client/server and cheaper hardware systems, make building a data warehouse a much more affordable exercise.

With the introduction of more powerful PCs and advances in software, data in the warehouse can be processed whenever a business user needs to analyse information. This concept, known as on-line analytical processing, or OLAP, means that up-to-date information is always available, so long as it resides in the data warehouse.

Another characteristic of an EIS is that data is stored and processed in a multi-dimensional format. This means that information can be viewed in a number of ways, so that interactions and relationships between data that are not obvious with conventional database tools can be identified and assessed. This can only be achieved by EIS. For example, a store might analyse sales of a particular product line by store, region or globally, enabling managers to identify anomalies in performance very quickly and in a high graphical format.

As the core application is commonly held on a powerful server, which undertakes the processing, with users accessing information from PCs connected across the corporate network, EIS is a prime example of an application based on a client/server principles.

The creation of a data warehouse takes considerable amount of management and planning to achieve successfully and, in the interim, the use of data access tools on the PC can provide a step towards the availability of the information needed to make the best business decisions.

10.13   Accessing Data

Next to its employees, data is the most important asset that a company has. Without data and easy access to it, a business cannot function properly.

When business computing systems were based on mainframes, virtually all data was stored centrally in a secure and well managed environment. Operators made
sure data was safe, secure and easily accessible by authorised users. They, also, carried out mundane, but nevertheless important, storage management functions such as data backup.

With the advent of distributed computer systems, such as client/server networks, this has changed. A large proportion of a business' data is now acquired, processed and stored throughout the enterprise on many PCs and file servers. This leads to duplication of effort, wasted resources, poor or non-existent disaster recovery planning and inconsistencies in data. Conversely, executives and managers have also changed the way they perceive data. When mainframes ruled, organisations saw little value in comparing information from different applications.

Even small organisations will hold data in a variety of formats. Sales information on one system, stock control on another, financial data elsewhere. Modern business systems require the analysis and comparison of this data. Executives and managers are now required to create sophisticated business plans, reports and presentations using data which might be located anywhere on the enterprise. They need to locate information intuitively and without complex computer instructions, retrieve and then integrate it with the systems they run on their own PC.

The need for greater control and improved security while enabling enterprise access to information has led to the concept of corporate data which can be accessed by any authorised user. Data mining is a term used to describe the process of sifting through data to identify trends and, therefore, opportunities. Data mining is used to extract information from the databases.

The data in a data warehouse is information created and used by an organisation's core business applications. Vast amounts of data exist in different forms and different databases, including traditional operational data, such as sales, cost, inventory, payroll and accounting data, external data such as industry sales, forecasts and macro-economic data. The data can also be meta-data, which is 'data about the data itself'.

Some data is in unstructured format, examples include electronic mail and bulletin board entries, letters and journal articles. The challenge is to organise, analyse and present this data in a manner meaningful to decision makers. The primary benefits of data mining are to determine the patterns among data elements and enable the summarising, categorising and analysis of data from almost any conceivable viewpoint.

Data mining provides a significant competitive edge beyond that available from traditional operational systems and allows the determination of patterns amongst products, customers and resources.

The latest data mining software can search across different databases. Seek out relevant data, interpret the format and then retrieve it into the desk-top applications used by executives and managers. The most advanced software of this type runs on PCs and incorporates graphical user interfaces such as Windows, or OS/2 for easy operation. Users can search for data using simple business language terms and keywords, then integrate it into their own programs for further processing, or manipulation.

Data warehousing and data mining are concepts which many organisations are working towards. However, there are also many simpler and powerful data tools on the market which can provide a fast solution to the problems of gathering and manipulating data from distributed platforms. In the absence of a data warehouse it is particularly important to consider the management aspects when using these tools, as users making uncontrolled queries can impact the mission-critical applications which run the business. This problem can be overcome by the selection of an appropriate tool with management facilities to control access, provide security for confidential data and to restrict uncontrolled queries on operational systems.

The concepts of data access, data warehousing and data mining are being used successfully by many organisations to gain insight into their customers. Implementing these technologies will enable staff to make informed decisions using the best quality information to ensure their organisation remains competitive, efficient and productive.

10.14   Re-engineering The Business

Business Process Re-engineering (BPR) is the strategic application of analysis and change at a departmental or corporate level to deliver business benefits such as cost savings and efficiency gains. Information technology is often applied to BPR projects, but it is not in itself the BPR. It is more accurately the method enabling business change.

Effective re-engineering starts with assessing operations at a corporate, departmental or even functional level. Each of the business processes involved is analysed to see how it works, how it interrelates with other processes, what it achieves and what it costs. The next stage is to investigate whether each process
is necessary and how it might be improved. Finally, new processes are developed and implemented so that improvements are made to overall

efficiency, with reduced costs and increased productivity. All of this can be achieved without any information technology whatsoever.

However, in most organisations it is likely that IT can be used to help automate certain processes, eliminate others and introduce new ways of working. For these reasons, it is closely associated with re-engineering and the allied area of workflow, which addresses the need to improve the management of the passage of information through an organisation. Software modelling tools can also aid the process of documenting business work flows in order that the processes are comprehensively understood before considering change.

The key benefits of the business process re-engineering are typically the elimination of wasteful or costly processes, improved customer service, better efficiency and higher productivity. However, BPR should not be viewed as the mere automation of existing processes. Effective BPR will eliminate the wasteful elements of the process and then, if it appropriate, apply systems to deliver the automation and better overall efficiency.

Many of the most successful re-engineering projects have involved the introduction of electronic or paperless trading. Banks and building societies have introduced document image processing, where forms and letters are converted to digital images and processes using computers and work flow practices. There is no need to handle paper. Work loads can be balanced and managed so that maximum productivity and responsiveness to customer requirements is achieved.

In the retail and industrial sectors, examination of the processes involved in the manufacturing and supply chains have led to the application of electronic commerce concepts to streamline the supply chain. Concepts such as Electronic Data Interchange (EDI) have been applied to speed up communications between trading partners, effect the rapid payment of invoices, reduce other lead times and eliminate the cost and potential of errors associated with handling and processing huge amounts of paper.

Organisations considering embarking on re-engineering projects are well advised to talk to consultants and solutions providers with widespread experience in business analysis and re-engineering. These are most likely to have the breath of skills to make a holistic assessment of business processes and to deliver cost effective solutions based on the best available practices and technologies. As with so many parts of business life, careful planning and a clear set of objectives are also essential

10.15   Systems In The Future

The diagram on the following page attempts to show the inter-relationship of various sciences and other academic fields, which includes computing and systems, not only as tools but as a science in its own right.

The illustration shows how easy it is for an experienced analyst to use a CASE tool to diagram nine different fields of any subject and their contributions to each other.

No attempt is made to indicate any firm relationships among the 'boxes'. This is an example of how various subject can function with each other and together, in order to exchange information of common interests.

Undoubtedly, computing has become one of the most important tools of modern times and will continue to be just as influential in the future, for ever and ever. Every student, pupil, academic, professional, at home or in the office, use it in order to show improvement in his/her work, to speed things up, to calculate or illustrate. The time will come when every human being will end up using a system, or develop a system to accommodate his/her thoughts, problems/solutions, methods, business, statistics and predictions.

With computerised systems, things can only improve. More education and training is required at the beginning of life, when children can understand and are able to hit the keyboard and use the systems. With an early introduction to computing, the conditions of current phobias of computers will only improve and within a generation, most probably eliminated.

Computers, their systems and their applications do not get rid of people. All they do is to improve life - imagine life without the computerised systems! After all computers as tools, systems used for a multiple of functions and applications for any kind of work, are only an extension of human brains, knowledge and experience.

It is hoped that the following diagram will prompt more inclusions and thoughts for the future. Computerised systems can be so enjoyable, in developing them, using them and playing with them.

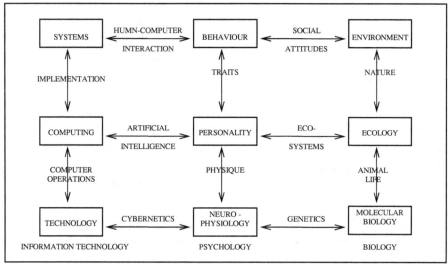

INTERRELATING SCIENCES DIAGRAM

11: The Millennium Bug

11.1 Year 2000 Compliance

The 'Millennium Problem' or 'Year 2000 Bug' has arisen due to the way that dates are stored, manipulated and interpreted by computers. When two digits are used to represent the year; for example 1997 represented as only '97', '00' could represent 1900 or 2000. This may cause some systems to malfunction after 31 December 1999, or sooner.

Systems which may fail due to the way dates are represented include those:

- Which assume '00' represents 1900 and not 2000,
- Not recognising 2000 as a leap year,
- Giving the date '99' special significance e.g. to represent contract end dates or expiry dates.

It is estimated that 80% of all computer systems will be affected by the Millennium problem and it will cost up to $600 billion world-wide to correct it (Gartner Group, 1996).

11.2 What Compliance Means

Most companies have adopted the British Standards Institution (BSI) definition of compliance.

In general terms, Year 2000 conformity means that neither the performance, nor functionality of a product, nor an item of equipment will be affected by dates before, during or after the year 2000. To ensure conformity, a number of conditions need to be met. One of these conditions is that year 2000 has to be recognised as a leap year. The others are listed below in this chapter.

11.3 General Integrity

General integrity ensures that the value used by any equipment or product for 'current date' will not cause any interruption in operation. If this condition is met, any increments in time (e.g. days, months, years or centuries) are always calculated correctly.

Prior to, during and after year 2000, date-based processes of any product or equipment must calculate, manipulate and represent dates correctly. No equipment or product can use particular date values which have been given special significance.

The century in any date used by interfaces and data storage systems must be specified:

- either explicitly, by using four digits or by including a century indicator,
- or by unambiguous algorithms or inferencing rules. For example, two-digits years greater than 50 imply 19xx, those with a value equal to or less tan 50 imply 20xx.

11.4 The Millennium Project Team

As a key player in a technology-driven sector, companies recognise the potential impacts of the year 2000 problem and the urgent need to address it. Some companies have already established a Millennium project team working toward year 2000 compliance.

Thus, the Millennium programme team should be responsible for:

- Managing the compliance initiative across all its business units on a global basis.
- Defining a project plan which ensures that any service provided and any systems that are used to deliver the service, will be compliant, as defined by the BSI definition of compliance.

- The impact assessment leading to the development of a year 2000 compliance solution, including a definition of all testing and implementation stages.
- A systems audit to establish which systems are affected by the problem. The team to prioritise internal systems, which will then be made compliant in order of priority.
- Suppliers audit, seeking year 2000 compliance statements and agreements from suppliers, requesting formal guarantees as to the compliance statement status of their products and services; monitoring their progress throughout.
- Questionnaires sent out and logging all answers onto a central database. Year 2000 standards also to be set for all future purchasers and developments. A company is committed to ensuring that all customers receive a secure and stable service up to and beyond the year 2000.

11.5 General Explanation

Problems can arise from some means of representing dates in computer equipment and products and from date-logic embedded in purchased goods or services, as the year 2000 approaches; during and after that year. As a result, equipment or products, including embedded control logic, may fail completely, malfunction or cause data to be corrupted.

To avoid such problems, organisations must check and modify, if necessary, internally produced equipment and products. Similarly check externally supplied equipment and products with their suppliers. Where checks are made with external suppliers, care should be taken to distinguish between claims of conformity and the ability to demonstrate conformity.

11.6 Conformity

As produced by British Standards Institution Technical Committee BDD1/-/3. Form reference DISC PD 2000-1 A definition of Year 2000 Conformity requirements.

Year 2000 conformity shall mean that neither performance, nor functionality is affected by dates prior to, during or after Year 2000. In particular, no value for current date will cause any interruption in operation. Date-based functionality must behave consistently for dates prior to, during and after Year 2000. In all interfaces and data storage, the century in any date must be specified either explicitly. Year 2000 must be recognised as a leap year.

Project 2000 must be set to achieve millennium compliance for all business processes. The programme must involve internal and external components, some with complex dependencies. Within the Project 2000 responsibilities, significant progress will be made by producing the required plans and in setting the appropriate policies for the planning procedures to be followed. To ensure the consistent use of the procedures, clear and concise plans supporting each process to be established for both, IT and embedded systems.

11.7 Year 2000 Risk Assessment Procedure

This section provides a formal risk assessment procedure for the year 2000 date compliance testing at an unfamiliar site or system. Additionally, the procedure expects systems analysis work to establish and record the system architecture.

The initial result of the work will be the production of a risk assessment report. The conclusions and recommendations provided in the report will influence the decision regarding possible further investigations and testing. The report will also influence the production of a test plan. Risk assessment in this instance is not the risk of year 2000 compliance failure, or the likelihood of failure. It is the risk that any such failure will create.

The risk assessment report should, therefore, cover the following risks:

- Risk to plant: The risk assessment report to show the extent of risk to plant, product and staff, if the system is not date compliant.
- Investigation risk: The risk created by the investigation and testing work required to determine year 2000 compliance.
- Correction risk: An assessment of the risks involved in correcting any year 2000 date problems to be made. This will cover the implications of errors or problems introduced by the correction changes.
- Other risks: The odd risks not covered by the above should be identified and assessed.
- Consequential damage: In all cases of identified risk, an assessment of the likely consequence should be made.
- Contingency plan: The assessment of risk must include an investigation on the contingency, or the disaster plan.

11.8 Objective Of Investigation

The primary objective of the year 2000 risk investigation is the production of a risk assessment report. This goal must in no way diminish the importance of ensuring the risk assessment exercise has no adverse impact on system operation.

11.8.1 Caution.

Use extreme caution in all respects during any visit; where possible do not touch the equipment. Get permission first and preferably ask the site personnel to do the touching.

11.8.2 Pre-visit Work

Before arranging a site visit, it is wise to acquire some knowledge of the operations personnel. Also, documentation such as functional specifications relating to the site should be obtained and reviewed before the visit. The pre-visit work is required as a familiarisation exercise. The visiting engineer must carry out some site research prior to the visit.

11.8.3 Site visit

A site visit appointment mutually convenient to the operations staff and engineer to be arranged. The visit should be agreed by telephone and confirmed in writing. The letter advises operations staff of the visit objective.

11.9 Top Down Analysis

Operations staff are very familiar with their systems and the primary task is the production of whatever product is manufactured at the plant. When you experience the site tour, you are likely to receive an overview of the production process rather than the architecture of the control equipment. The initial task should be a top down analysis of the plant.

11.10 Taking Notes

A structured analysis is difficult to make when the information presented is bottom up. The best way to deal with this situation is to ask questions and steer the tour in the direction you require. Make notes and at the end of the tour document the findings with diagrams and in a structured manner.

All relevant material should be copied, or borrowed and used in the production of the risk assessment report. Further site visits may be required as a result of the documentation inspection and resultant research.

11.11 Reporting Risks

This will be the most important section of the risk assessment report. The assessment of risk relates to the harm that may occur at the problem dates identified.

When the assessment information is presented, a person or persons will use this material during the decision making process for this particular piece of equipment. No testing will be carried out unless a formal decision based on a risk assessment report has previously been made.

11.12 Year 2000 Vulnerability

If the system being assessed is found to be without any concept of date then the risk is as low as can be and testing for compliance is not required.

If a system cannot be guaranteed to be free of date processing software then it must be assumed to be present. At the very least the findings will be documented and can be referenced, should future problems occur.

11.13 Consequence Of Non-compliance

The detailed commercial consequential loss assessment exercise is beyond the scope of the risk assessment, but if a significant loss of product or raw material

is likely, then this should be stated. The objective is to provide adequate information for an informed decision to be made regarding any future testing.
If everything looks fine, but there is a rusty water tank positioned above the master station that looks about to burst, then this is a good point which must be reported. This may not have direct date compliance implications, but it will influence the decision to conduct invasive investigations and tests.

11.14 Quality Assessment

The risk assessment exercise will provide an opportunity for the equipment general condition to be established.

The objective here is to provide information to whoever has the task of deciding what should be done to a given system. If the quality assessment shows the system is in a good state of repair then invasive investigations may be considered appropriate. If the continued operation of the system is considered miraculous then perhaps a different approach will be taken.

The decision regarding what will be done with the system will be based on the risk assessment document, therefore, the quality assessment section is very important. A degree of subjectivity will result here, but this is acceptable.

11.15 Recommendations On Planning

Where appropriate, recommendations should be made to assist in planning for the next stage. Principally, this relates to issues of year 2000 compliance testing, but any other matter deemed relevant should be covered.

The recommendations made will be considered when the next stage is planned and should be as wide ranging as necessary.

11.16 Conclusion On The Millennium Bug

Like any other business project, an organisation must gain enough understanding in how to deal with the millennium problem. Some systems and equipment may be free of the millennium bug, but no one can be sure until they have been rigorously assessed and tested. It is well worth contacting the supplier to ask whether the technical environment is year 2000 compliant. Older versions will almost certainly not be able to handle the date change.

Companies that have got a clean bill of health should tell the customers. This will definitely assist in improving the sales of their equipment and products.

12: Project Planning

12.1 Managing The Plan

There are many PC-based tools and software which help with the management of a project and the allocation of responsibilities to software engineers. For the examples of the plans in this chapter, the PMW package has been used. It must be noted that the selection of a package depends on what the IT department's study has highlighted; the usage and tasks the project control software package is supposed to cover.

The stages of development and the steps within each stage are recorded, together with the timescales and the staff involved. A Gantt chart is produced showing the dates applicable to the steps completed and those outstanding. The updating is done regularly, preferably once a week and all participants become the recipients of various reports. Meetings are then held to discuss outstanding tasks, or issues arising.

12.2 Project Control

To maintain an effective project control, the overall planning activity is supported by the project managers. The management forum sets priorities, allocates resources, resolves issues and deals with risks.

12.2.1 Planning Function
The planning function relies on receiving up-to-date plans from individual project managers. As such, the planning office is responsible for the overall plan and the identification of risks and issues. Further on, the individual project plans, their monitoring, the transference of the actual resources and the reporting are handled by the planning office.

12.2.2 Initiation And Maintenance Of Plans.
The plans are initiated by the Project Manager. These are then set up by the Planner. Once approved, the plans are maintained by the Planning/Project Office. The Planning Office personnel define the standards. Additionally, the planners are responsible for the development and maintenance of the integrated baseline plan.

12.2.3 Plans For Management
Vital to the effective management of the programme are the plans with milestones, which:
- Set priorities,
- Allocate resources,
- Highlight issues,
- Assist in managing risks.

12.2.4 Time Recording
Timesheets are submitted on a weekly basis by the individuals in the project teams. Their completion is checked by the Project Manager. The details entered in the timesheets are transferred on the plans as actuals. The status of the plans is monitored by the Planning Office.

12.2.5 Reviews
Regular reviews are held with the Project Managers. Following the reviews, the planner makes the necessary adjustments to the plans. When the adjustments are completed, copies with the appropriate changes are submitted to the Project Managers for approval.

12.3 Quality Of Plans

The quality of the overall plan depends on the state of the plans of the individual teams and the commitment of the Project Managers to support this approach. With the outputs generated, the Project Manager identifies the resource requirements, the skills required to meet the targets and the costs incurred within the approved budget.

12.3.1 Plans Assurance
The Project Managers ensure that the:
- Plans are fit for the project,
- Current plans are logged,
- Plans and work completed match the project deadlines,
- Plans show adequate resources,

- Progress to date is in line with the expectations.

12.3.2 Project Activities
The project activities can include all the:
- IT applications,
- Embedded systems,
- Infrastructure,
- Equipment.

12.4 Planning Office Preparations

The Planning Office is responsible for the:
- Consistent standards on plans,
- Site plans development and maintenance,
- Agreement on milestones,
- Baselining of plans against actuals,
- Inter-projects dependencies.

12.4.1 The Planner
The Planner works with individual Project Managers for the:
- Estimated and actual project costing,
- Planning training needs for the project teams,
- Monitoring of progress against milestones,
- Identification of contentions,
- Project issues and risks,
- Proposes solutions and corrective actions.

12.4.2 Deliverables
The planning tool deliverables include the:
- Plans with milestones (based on the individual team plans),
- A register of issues and risks and their impact on target dates.

12.4.3 Monitoring
The monitoring by the Planning Office enables the:
- Viewing,
- Tracking,
- Reporting.

12.4.3.1 Viewing:
- Production of Gantt charts,
- Fields to create new plans,
- Gantt by resource,
- Viewing of dependencies,
- Creation of new resources,
- Setting up and viewing of fixed loading patterns,
- Assigning of categories.

12.4.3.2 Tracking:
- Hours worked from time sheets,
- Actual end dates, Status and Complete,
- Timesheet per person,
- Timesheets for all resources,

12.4.3.3 Reporting:
- Gantt chart at task level,
- Gantt chart at phase level,

- Actuals against baseline effort,
- All project milestones,
- Total loading of resources in days per week,
- Tracked time by week,
- Estimate to complete,
- Subtotals by project within group.

12.5 Settings

In addition, the planner prepares all plans to show the following settings:
- Project,
- Phase activity,
- Task,
- Milestone.

12.5.1 Outputs
Based on these settings the Planning Office outputs the following:
- Check list,
- Hierarchical chart,
- Programme flowchart,
- Weekly timesheets modifications,
- Individual project plans,
- Main plan.

12.5.2 The Stages
The various stages of work within the projects are classified by site. Systems and tasks are allocated within the stages.

12.5.3 Tasks
The tasks for the testing of the systems are uniform to all of the plans in the projects. These are:
- Investigation,
- Risk Assessment,
- Review,
- Site Test Plan,
- Contingency Plan,
- Test,
- Documentation,
- Sign off.

12.5.4 Actuals
The actuals recorded are based on the entry from the timesheets received from the Project Managers.

12.5.5 Baseline
The start and end dates are locked and baselined. The baselining on the plans are:
- Non-production time,
- General project time,
- General project management tasks,
- Activities.

12.5.6 Milestones
Where visits or tests on the sites have been completed, they are marked as milestones on the plans. Milestones are agreed with the Project Managers.

12.5.7 Tracked Time And Estimates
Based on the project managers' assumptions, estimates are entered on the plans. These estimates are initially baselined to show variances. The actuals are compared against these estimates.

12.5.8 Resource Loading

All resources are allocated on the planned tasks. To enable quick tracking of loading, the resources are uniquely abbreviated.

12.5.9 Sub-totals

The following sub-totals can be extracted from any of the project plans:

- Resource loading,
- Elapsed time against phases,
- Sites,
- Systems.

12.6 Planner's Responsibilities

The following responsibilities are part of the planning service offered by the individual planners to the project in general:

- Liaison with Project Managers,
- Co-ordination of all plans,
- Equal responsibility to all teams,
- Regular reviews with all Project Managers,
- Individual reviews,
- Global reviews (of all plans, at least every three months),
- Ad hoc presentations,
- Monitoring of:
  - -Actuals,
  - -Appropriate dates,
  - -Project milestones,
  - -All planning modifications.
- Training on planning:
  - -Filtering,
  - -Production of plans,
  - -Timesheet entries,
  - -Conversions.
- Collection of all estimates:
  - -Resource,
  - -Costs,
  - -Timescales.

12.7 Planning Objectives

The objective of using a planning tool, such as the Microsoft Project, PMW, or spreadsheets, is to produce plans and reports based on details submitted by the Project Managers. Some plans may already exist in a draft format, at detailed and summary level.

12.7.1 Plan Completeness

The completeness of the plans at the end of each period largely relies upon the input from the project teams. The Planner's responsibility is to verify the plans received and consequently standardise, rationalise and consolidate the plans entered by the individuals.

12.7.2 Standards

All project plans can be developed to a constant standard. Although there is a certain degree for local site control, the milestones can be agreed and all project plans can be baselined and monitored against actuals.

12.8 Policies

The planner demonstrates and advises on what already exists on the planning tool/s. Any changes to the planning practices rely on policy decisions made by senior management.

Bibliography

A Sofroniou, The Management Of Commercial Computing, PsySys Limited, ISBN: 0 9527956 0 4.

A Sofroniou, Structured Management Techniques, Association For Psychological Counselling And Training, Training Material, 1984.

A Sofroniou, Structured Systems Methodologies, Published and unpublished lecture notes, 1987 -1997.

A Sofroniou, Management Styles lectures, 1982.

A Sofroniou, Thesis submission on Automotive Components and Materials Purchasing System for Engineering Qualifications, 1983.

A Sofroniou, Collaborative project on Knowledge-base, Expert Systems and Artificial Intelligence, with Imperial College, Logica plc and The Engineering Industry Training Board, 1985-1986.

A Sofroniou, Rapid Structured Methodology for Life Assurance Systems, 1990-1992.

A Sofroniou, Analysis and Design project on EPoS Retail and Logistic System, 1995.

A Sofroniou, Research project, a study on COTS (Commercial Off The Shelf) Packages, 1995.

A Sofroniou, Technical Design projects for Internet Integration, Security, Client/Servers, Data Warehousing and Databases, 1996-1997.

A Sofroniou, The Year 2000 Project and Planning Procedures for European Group of Companies, 1998.

Ian Graham, Object Oriented Methods, Addison Wesley, ISBN: 0 201 56521 8.

James Martin, James Odell, Object Oriented Analysis and Design, Prentice Hall, ISBN: 0 13 630245 9.

David A Taylor, Object Oriented Technology: A Manager's Guide, Addison Wesley, ISBN: 0 201 56358 4.

E Yourdon and L Constantine, Structured Design, Yourdon inc., 1975.

Chris Gane and Trish Sarson, Structured Systems Analysis: Tools and Techniques, Improved System Technologies, Inc., 1977.

J L Alty and M J Coombs, Expert Systems Concepts and Examples, NCC Publications, ISBN: 0 85012 399 2.

G L Simons, Introducing Microprocessors, NCC Publications, ISBN: 0 85012 209 0.

CCTA (Central Computer and Telecommunications Agency), SSADM and PRINCE (PRoject IN Controlled Environment) Methodology, publicly available open products.

Action 2000. Millennium Bug Campaign, DTI (Department of Trade and Industry), 1998.

Profile

ANDREAS SOFRONIOU IS A PRACTISING PSYCHOTHERAPIST, AN EXECUTIVE WITH INTERNATIONAL ORGANISATIONS AND AN ADVISER TO GOVERNMENTS. HIS PUBLISHED BOOKS INCLUDE INFORMATION TECHNOLOGY, MANAGEMENT, PSYCHOLOGY, POETRY, PHILOSOPHY, AND FICTION.

Career:

During his varied career, Andreas held the positions of Chief Executive Officer, Programmes Director, Managing Director, Overseas Marketing Executive, Production and Inventory Manager, Group Senior Systems Consultant, European Systems Manager, and Principal Technical Adviser with the multi-national organisations of EDS, PsySys, International Computers Limited (ICL), Pitney Bowes, Plessey (GEC), Raychem (Tyco) and the Engineering Industry Training Board (EITB).

For four years, the Global Programmes Director for EDS (Electronic Data Systems), the largest outsourcing international organisation. For twenty years, the Managing Director of PsySys Limited. a consultancy responsible for the development of systems, management and people. Many of EDS and PsySys clients are international companies, software houses, European Union Commissions and British Government Departments.

Education:

Andreas holds the degrees of Doctor of Psychology, Executive MBA and Doctor of Science. He is a Life Fellow of the Institute of Directors, and a chartered fellow member of eighteen professional institutions for Engineering, Systems, Computing, Complementary Medicine, Management, Production, Programming, Marketing, Petroleum, Data Processing, Psychotherapy, and Counselling.

Other studies included Children's Art and Psychotherapy, Mental Illness/Mental Health and Advanced Psychological Topics. Andreas established his first therapeutic clinic in 1973. Since then, he continued practising as a Psychoanalyst, Psychotherapist, Counsellor and Philosophical Therapist in various cities of the United Kingdom. Andreas is the current President of the Association for Psychological Counselling and Training, a position held since 1982.

For the last twenty years, a Research Life Fellow, Professor, and a member of working parties in the United Kingdom, European Union, and American Institutes for Information Technology, Management, and Therapy.

Publications:

Many of his research papers and articles were published during his participation as an Information Technology expert, where he represented Britain to the European Union and as a practitioner of therapeutic psychology at the Institute of Psychology and Parapsychology, and the Harley Street Centre, London.

A published author of twenty fiction and non-fiction books, the subjects include Information Technology, Management, Computing, Systems, Risks Management, Change Management, Psychology, Therapy, Counselling, Poetry, and Philosophy. Some of his books and articles were also published on the Internet for the international readership. For a list of publications please visit:

http://www.publishedauthors.net/sofroniou and http://www.lulu.com/sofroniou.

Awards:

For achievements in Systems Engineering, Psychology and Directing, Andreas' biographical records are included in the directory of 'Who's Who in the World', published by Marquis of America and other international biographical publications.

In 2001, Andreas was nominated for the House of Lords membership (non-political) and subsequently was bestowed with the Scottish nobility title of The Laird of Glencairn, and his wife with the title of Lady, the Laird of John O'Groats.

In January 2003, Andreas and PsySys Limited received the Achievement Award for twenty years of continued growth and client satisfaction.

In March 2004, Andreas received the EDS award for Distinguished Global Services with the Company.

Description

There can be little doubt that information systems and computing in general, will become increasingly important in the years ahead. This book is, therefore, aiming to fill a gap in the current business and tutorial literature.

The Business Information Systems book has been designed for the business person, for the student and the computer professional who needs a detailed overview of Information Technology and the systems involved.

The book explores the fundamental aspects of operational computing, the development of new information systems, the choice of packages and the structured methodologies used. Current systems are discussed according to their structure and the book focuses on further developments in information technology, the year 2000 compliance and their planning.

In writing the book, the author is mostly concerned with the development and the managing of systems and people in multi-national corporations, software houses, government departments, the European Union Commissions and academia.

EurIng Dr Andreas Sofroniou has close links with business systems and their development, as well as the system engineering profession as a whole. He has developed numerous systems and managed a variety of applications and systems people, including Year 2000 projects.

It is the author's wish that the reader thoroughly enjoys reading the contents of this book.

ISBN: 0 9527956 0 4

Copyright © Andreas Sofroniou

1996 - Revised in 2000.

Published and Printed by:

PsySys Limited, 33, SN3 1PH, UK.

Price: **£17.50**

www.ingramcontent.com/pod-product-compliance
Lightning Source LLC
Chambersburg PA
CBHW051252050326
40689CB00007B/1169